MW01051142

THE

THE

WILD + FREE
FAMILY

ALSO BY
AINSLEY ARMENT

THE CALL OF THE WILD + FREE

WILD + FREE BOOK CLUB

WILD + FREE NATURE

WILD + FREE HOLIDAYS

WILD + FREE HANDCRAFTS

THE
WILD + FREE
FAMILY

*Forging Your Own Path to
a Life Full of Wonder,
Adventure, and Connection*

AINSLEY ARMENT

HarperOne
An Imprint of HarperCollinsPublishers

HarperCollins books may be purchased for educational, business, or sales promotional use. For information, please email the Special Markets Department at SPsales@harpercollins.com.

FIRST EDITION

Designed by Janet Evans-Scanlon

Illustrations:
Pages i, iv–v (background), 11, 15, 23, 33, 56, 69, 83, 99, 103, 106–7, 111, 127, 142, 159, 160, 170, 182, 197, 206–7, 211: Julia Dreams/Creative Market
Pages iii, iv (house and hearts), 1, 8, 10, 24, 34, 43, 57, 72, 77, 78, 82, 94, 100, 118, 125 (hearts), 128, 165, 176, 181, 186, 189, 193, 201, 209: Redchocolate/ Creative Market
Pages 7, 157: KitVector/Creative Market
Pages 18, 169, 173: Ruslana Vasiukova/Creative Market
Pages 21, 84: Hello Talii/Creative Market
Pages 28, 65, 135: Lucia Fox/Creative Market
Page 51: Ylivdesign/Creative Market
Pages 89, 143: Vectorstockersland/Creative Market
Pages 113, 204: cloudstreetlab/Creative Market
Page 125 (RV): Alex Krugli/Creative Market

Library of Congress Cataloging-in-Publication Data has been applied for.

ISBN 978-0-06-299823-1

22 23 24 25 26 LSC 10 9 8 7 6 5 4 3 2 1

To Ben—
sun to my moon
filling me
with light
illuminating me
with love

To Wyatt, Dylan, Cody, Annie, and Millie—
the brightest stars
teaching me
forever
leading me
to wonder

Contents

Introduction

YOUR FAMILY
WAS MADE FOR MORE

n the spring of 2009, my husband Ben and I were at a crossroads. We had moved to Atlanta, Georgia, for a job opportunity and were enjoying a comfortable life. We had two little boys at the time and another on the way. We lived in a cookie-cutter house with two cars in the driveway and an opportunity to purchase a new home that summer.

Our son Wyatt was in a four-day-a-week prekindergarten, and I took our three-year-old, Dylan, to the gym each morning, where he played in the childcare center while I worked out.

I was building a small nutrition business in my spare time and running a blog for mothers called *Chattahoochee Mama*, a tongue-in-cheek nod to the famous river that ran near our house.

I was content. Ben was content. My children were happy. And our home was peaceful.

But our family was missing the one thing that would make each day feel like something more than going through the motions: a greater purpose for our lives together.

We spent those warm Georgia evenings at the park, where our boys played while Ben and I tried to decide whether to double-down on the job, purchase a home here, and settle for life in suburbia.

We wrestled with the decision. Staying put would mean surrendering our dreams on the altar of security. But walking away would mean giving up everything we had ever worked for: a good job, a nice house, and a sense of financial security for the first time in our lives.

In the meantime, I went through the motions of taking Wyatt to school each morning. I remember sitting in the drop-off carpool line with my numbered security card on the back of the sun visor so they could identify him.

As I approached the drop-off point, a teacher would fling open the van door, scoop Wyatt out of his car seat like a parachutist going out the back of a C-17, and yell "Go, go, go!" while I frantically blew him a kiss, tossed out a sack lunch, and kept the van rolling to avoid holding up the line.

At the time, I was driving an old minivan that was not equipped with automatic doors like most everyone else's newer models. The teacher would invariably leave the door open, thinking I would push the button to close it, only to leave me with no choice but to drive away with the door wide open, no matter the weather. I would pull over on the side of a busy, two-lane road, get out, walk around the side of the van, and close it with a big heave-ho.

It would have been funny if it hadn't happened every single day.

It's not that we didn't have beauty and blessings in our lives, making memories and marking the milestones with gratitude. But in many ways, it felt like our life was being lived for us.

We were like the Jetsons cartoon family, who get scooped out of their beds by conveyer belts each morning and transported to the bathroom for a shower, to the closet to get dressed, and to the kitchen to eat breakfast before being taken to work in flying cars. Only our conveyor belt was the school schedule, the work routine, the gym membership, and the daily grind.

Unless we did something about it, nothing would ever change. This routine would become our life until death do us part.

One day at work, Ben got called into a meeting with the other directors at his company. The company was making cutbacks, and the CEO asked each of them to write down the names of the employees who should be let go first, the low performers. Ben's heart sank. These were the very people he worked with, ate lunch with, and celebrated with.

He said it felt like nominating tributes in *The Hunger Games*.

After the exercise, the CEO dismissed everyone but the top executives. As Ben walked back to his office, passing the very employees whose names had been jotted on the whiteboard, he had a sudden realization: there was nothing stopping the CEO from writing down *his* name after he left the meeting.

The job security that was keeping us from making courageous decisions, following our dreams, going on adventures, and spending more time together as a family was nothing more than an illusion. We realized that we had built our lives around supporting someone else's purpose—the company's purpose, society's purpose, the school system's purpose. But we weren't living *our* purpose.

I don't recommend this to everyone, but we decided to quit that life without any other prospects and move back to Virginia Beach, where we had always dreamed of raising a family, close to the ocean and the ones we loved. We cast off society's conventions to build a life based on what mattered most to us. Time together. Our own schedule. And the freedom to travel the world at will.

It wasn't easy. In fact, it took several years to find our footing. But after a few different endeavors, some successful, some not, we finally found our purpose, which led me to start an Instagram account and later an organization called Wild + Free.

With dozens of events each year, hundreds of thousands of community members, millions of podcast downloads, groups all over the world, and the creation of the Wild + Free Farm Village in the Allegheny Mountains of Virginia, Wild + Free has become a movement of families who share the same heart and are breaking free from society's pressures and building a more authentic life.

The Life We Built Together

My family's move back to my hometown proved to be providential. Our contract on a home purchase fell through without any explanation, and we couldn't understand why the seller wouldn't sign the agreement. But then my mother was diagnosed with a malignant brain tumor, and it all became clear.

We were meant to move into her home to look after her and my brother, who was battling his own chronic illness. Now that she's gone, my mother's home has become our own, and my brother still lives in our care.

It's not the life I thought we would be living. It's not the one we always dreamed about. But it's the life we have, and it has come to impact our family in some pretty profound ways, from the intimate moments we had with my mother before she passed away to being close to the ocean for countless seaside explorations.

It has also taught us some priceless lessons. It's taught us that although it might be easier to outsource care, we develop strength in character by caring for others—the widows, the orphans, and the unwell. It has given us the chance to show our children what it means to be there for family members at their worst, to lean into hard things instead of running away.

In many ways, it has also helped us stay connected to my mother, even though my two little girls were never able to meet her. She passed away before they were born, and yet the yearning to know her still beats strong in their hearts. When they were much younger, whenever they met an older woman who visited our house, they would ask me, "Is that my grandmother?"

My daughter Annie often asks me about my mother. She loves to hear stories about what she was like as a mom to me, and she always concludes wistfully, "I wish I could meet her."

Little do they know that each and every day they walk the same halls my mother used to walk. They sleep in the same bedroom where she tucked me into bed each night. And they eat at the kitchen table where my mother served countless meals and stayed up late to drink tea and talk with me after a night out.

They are walking in her footsteps and experiencing her legacy, whether they know it or not.

On the other hand, living this life means forgoing what could have been. A bedroom for each of our kids, instead of stacking them three to a room. A neighborhood with other children who are the same age. Living near our other family members so our children could have grandparents as a regular part of their lives.

It's tempting to look back and wonder if we should have done things differently. Should we have moved to Colorado when we had the chance? Should we have never left my hometown so that I could have noticed my mother's symptoms and perhaps gotten her treatment before it was too late? Should we have pursued a different occupation to avoid the pressures that rattled our marriage early on?

Life can feel like a "choose your own adventure" story with feelings of regret and remorse, gratitude and glee, over the choices we've made and the circumstances that have defined us. It would be easy to regret so many decisions gone wrong.

But no, this is the life we built together, and for better or for worse, I will be eternally grateful for it. This is the life we were meant to live. For such a time as this.

My story isn't your story. Our journey isn't your own.

But maybe we aren't so different. Maybe we hope for similar things.

If we don't reimagine what our families can be, we will miss the opportunity to give our children what they need. When we assume that a family has to look a certain way or function according to a specific form, we miss the opportunity to build a meaningful and fulfilling life together.

This practice of life-building feels largely outside our control, but I assure you that it's not. We may not be able to fix the behavior of an absent spouse. We may not be able to change a medical diagnosis, a tragic past, or a decision gone wrong. And we may not be able to fix the problems outside our doors, but we can cultivate a culture that's true to ourselves within our own homes.

My friend Cindy Rollins, the author of *Mere Motherhood*, shared this sentiment about homeschooling, but it could just as easily be said about our family's life together: "It isn't the big plans that are going to make your homeschool. It is the little things you do faithfully year after year that are going to add up to an education and a life for your children."[1]

In the absence of doing great things, you can do small things with great love:

The making of meals and folding of laundry.

The reading of books and explaining of algebra.

The planning of lessons and creating of moments.

The making of handcrafts and taking of nature walks.

The searching for lost lovies and finding of favorite toys.

The games you play and the puzzles you build.

The smile you flash when your child looks up.

The hug you give when your spouse walks by.

The tired prayers you pray.

The grieving tears you cry.

The magic of this life isn't found in the hustle and bustle of constant activity but in the intentional, ordinary decisions of our days.

Keep Fighting for the Light

Your ideal family culture can sometimes feel like an elusive will-o'-the-wisp that you're chasing through the forest, hoping it will lead you to a hidden wonder. Instead, it takes you through sinking sands, blazing deserts, and raging rivers until you're lost, alone, and feeling defeated.

In the end, it feels like folklore. So you give up.

This generation of wild and free families is different, though. I sensed it seven years ago when a group of misfit mamas gathered at the first Wild + Free retreat to connect over common ideals. These were parents longing to connect with their children in a different way. And now, after more than a dozen conferences have brought women to their knees with passionate tears and a desire to change the future of their families, I can honestly say that this idea of living wild and free is more than a passing fad.

It is a movement that is sweeping through homes and finding its way into the very depths of our souls. It is becoming a part of our DNA, a trait we will pass on to our children and our children's children.

It is awaking a generation to a new way of living—so fiercely and vulnerably that it feels scary and uncertain and oh so real. Yet despite embarking on unchartered territory, not one of us is willing to turn back. We may not know where we're heading, but we are trusting that it's worth it.

If there is one thing that can and will be said of this generation of parents, it is that we did not go gentle into that good night, as the poet Dylan Thomas wrote.[2]

Every day, I see mothers and fathers fighting for the families they desire. I see broken adults committing to raise whole children. I see brave parents doing the hard work of healing from their own childhood trauma and breaking generational cycles. And I witness family after family reclaiming childhood and restoring what has been lost.

If you are in the trenches and wondering if what you are doing is worth it, please know that it is. Keep raging against the dying of the light, my friend.

It's time to find your way back to where you belong. Back to the purpose of your family being knit together. Back to the

passions that stir your soul and the mission to help your children become whole. You are not just breaking cycles for yourself or your children, but for generations to come.

This isn't a book about how to become a better family. It isn't a self-help book on how to become a proficient parent. And it certainly isn't a book about finding financial freedom or starting a business.

The chapters in front of you offer personal stories from me and other wild and free families, along with research meant to give you permission to cast aside convention and invite you to live a more meaningful, adventurous life.

> My good friend Lydia once told me, "It is always better to do hard and important things together. But if no one else is willing, following your calling is still worth doing, even if you have to do it alone."

My intent is to share my story and the many resources, values, and circumstances that have changed our family for the better—the way we live, the way we parent, and the way we love. Your family was made for more, and in each chapter, we'll unpack one aspect of what your family was made *for*, why it matters, and how you might explore living that out in your unique situation.

Whether you travel full-time, homeschool, unschool, or traditionally school your children . . . whether you work for yourself or someone else . . . whether you live in an apartment in the city, in a single-family home in suburbia, or on a homestead on a hill . . . whether you're a single parent, a couple on the rocks, or in a thriving marriage—this is a book about carving your own wild path in the midst of modern culture and, in doing so, finding more love and joy in the way you relate to each other as a family.

My hope is that your family will be inspired to love stronger, live more fully, and grow closer to each other. My prayer is that you will be emboldened to repair relationships and break generational patterns for your children and your children's children. My ultimate desire is that your family will become wild and free.

I am so honored to walk among you, hear your stories, and encourage the incredible, brave work you are doing. Together we will break chains and set souls free.

Let's do this.

1

TO CREATE
A FAMILY CULTURE

I do think that families are the most
beautiful things in all the world!

—JO MARCH IN *LITTLE WOMEN*
BY LOUISA MAY ALCOTT

Your family has a culture, whether you choose one or not. This might sound obvious, but we're often too preoccupied with life to pay much attention to it. We get too wrapped up in living, too exhausted to care. If you do not choose your own family culture, one will be assigned to you by society at large. This often looks like both parents working nine-to-five jobs and the kids confined within four walls at school all day, having their heads crammed full of standardized information that neither takes into account their intrinsic human needs nor makes room for their diverse intelligence, personalities, or possible neurodivergence.

Most of us already know this from dating in high school or from choosing random home-repair contractors on the internet, but *not* being intentional doesn't mean we're *not* making a decision. By leaving our family culture to happenstance, we are very much determining how it will be.

We have a choice in how our children are raised, what their education is like, what kind of parents they have, and what the story of their childhoods will be when they come to the sunset of their lives.

Maybe you've started to hear a quiet whisper beckoning you to reclaim the culture of your family. It starts as a still, small voice but grows louder and stronger for those who have the ears to hear it.

Your family culture reflects your values, your vision, and your varied interests. It creates a vernacular for the invisible. And it gives every member the vocabulary to use and understand what you are about.

By reclaiming your family culture, you can give your kids the gift of a childhood.

You can give them the gift of time to discover their own passions.

You can give them a future free from past brokenness.

You can give them back their family.

What Is a Family Culture?

Before we get too far, let's nail down a definition. A family culture is your values and vision, your interests and traditions, all wrapped up in one. It's how you structure your life together. How you spend your time each day. The friends you have. The job you hold and how that impacts your family.

It's where you go on vacation and what you do on your days off. How you speak to each other. The traditions you keep. How much media you consume and where you spend your money.

How you show love through discipline. How you handle conflict. And how quickly you forgive one another.

It's whether you dance in the kitchen, make breakfast for dinner, and play board games at night. It's how early you rise, the books you read aloud at bedtime, and whether you dim the lights or turn them up when company comes over. It's whether you say I love you when you hang up the phone.

A family culture is the sum total of a parent's decisions— both conscious and unconscious—and the circumstances that result from it. Sometimes those circumstances are intended; other times they're not.

A family culture starts with a vision: a picture of what you want it to be. It becomes your North Star, guiding the decisions you make and providing a helpful navigation for what you will or will not do.

As a teenager, I often worked as a babysitter and got to observe firsthand what I didn't like about other family cultures, like the ones where children were meant to be seen but not heard.

I remember what happened when a six-year-old girl interrupted her mother while she was speaking to another adult in a waiting room. The mother looked at her sharply and said, "Now, darling, you remember what to do if you want to speak to me. You touch my arm, so I know that you're there. I'll respond when I am finished speaking."

The timid girl started to speak again, but the mother held up a stiff finger before continuing her conversation. I have no doubt the mother meant well, to endow her daughter with the gift of social cues. But she failed to see the frantic look in her daughter's face.

The next minute, the poor girl stood there in a puddle of her own urine, humiliated. She had desperately needed to use the bathroom.

Then there were the families where the kids were treated like adults, rather than equals with different needs. They were allowed to watch R-rated movies and play violent video games. The parents freely cussed in front of their kids and drank too much out of a sense that they were just "one of the gang."

I remember attending a New Year's Eve party in middle school where the parents brought a cooler of beer upstairs for us kids to drink while the adults partied downstairs. I admit, I preferred being around this kind of family culture because it felt freer than being tight-lipped and walking around on eggshells. That is, until I realized it was robbing us of a childhood on the other end of the spectrum.

I remember the homes that felt warm and connected and those that felt chaotic and isolating. I remember families I admired and those I felt sorry for.

I'm sure you have your own experiences too.

What we don't realize is that each of these family cultures didn't happen by accident. They are formed by small acts of intention (or lack of intention), one day at a time.

Creating a Family Culture

Most of us want a family culture that reflects the best parts of our own childhoods. We want our kids to love the movies we watched, the vacations we took, and the experiences we enjoyed.

If we're completely honest, we want them to have *our* childhoods.

For me, it was watching *Anne of Green Gables* on repeat, having sleepovers with friends, riding bikes until dusk, reading books in the tree house, and spending summer vacations in Ocean City, New Jersey.

For my husband, it was riding BMX, shooting a basketball in the driveway, playing flag football with friends, starting a lawn-mowing business, and getting involved with the church youth group.

And yet none of those things has ever interested our children. They don't want *our* childhoods. They want their own.

Our kids love riding four-wheelers, making music, writing novels, and enjoying pizza and a movie on Friday nights with the whole family. They save unopened Lego sets in hopes that they'll appreciate in value over time. And they wouldn't know what to do with themselves without our annual Wild + Free Family Camp and other travels throughout the year.

There are things our children contribute to our family culture, such as game nights, talent shows, and having medieval battles with foam weapons. And there are things we contribute, like travel adventures, dinners together no matter what, and constantly working to clear our schedule, not fill it.

We may not be able to replicate our own childhoods, but we can create a family culture out of the unique personalities and passions we have as a family. We can decide what our family story will be.

When it comes to creating a family culture, there are negotiables and nonnegotiables. A nonnegotiable is something that doesn't offer choices. We don't have a lot of these, and we try to make them invitations rather than demands. But as nonnegotiables, they are what they are.

For example, all members of our family are expected to eat dinner together. Everyone has a few simple chores (or "team get-tos," as I like to call them) at the beginning and end of each day. And we have high standards for how we treat and speak to each other. We're far from perfect in this area, but it's a value we constantly impart and strive to live out.

We have a few more nonnegotiables, but you get the idea.

A negotiable is something that allows flexibility. Some afternoons, I start reading aloud in the living room for anyone who wants to show up. Participation is not mandatory, and yet it fills my heart with joy to see the kids (and even the dog) gather round. (I serve treats to make this time more inviting.)

In our family, being homeschooled is a negotiable. We want our kids to have a say in where and how they are educated, and each year, so far, they have chosen to stay the course.

Living our values doesn't play out perfectly. With so many people, personalities, and preferences vying for their way, our families can feel messy and chaotic much of the time. On top of this, family culture leaks. We have to be relentless defenders of our culture if we are to stave off the forces of apathy and misplaced priorities that threaten it. If we're not vigilant, we can lose our way.

A family culture is the natural outflow of your values, which sometimes show up in unexpected ways. I recently accepted a Friday-evening dinner invitation for our family that preempted our weekly pizza-and-movie night. When I told the kids, you would have thought that I had just canceled Christmas. Note to self: protect those weekly rituals the kids value so much.

Live your values, and your family culture will fall into place.

Determining your family culture is the final frontier in our modern age. It's the last remaining place where you can stake your claim. And you can do it without moving to the borderlands of Alaska with the crazies, criminals, and counterculturists (although that doesn't sound entirely unappealing).

You can do it right where you live. You only need to endure the questions and comments of those who don't understand why you're not living like everyone else.

Being wild and free isn't for the faint of heart.

Here are some questions to help you discover your own family culture. Feel free to discuss these with your spouse or your entire family. Write down your answers and return to them again and again:

1. What families have inspired you by their lifestyle choices? In what way?

2. What are some family cultures you'd like to avoid? Why are they undesirable?

3. What were the best parts of your own childhood? How about the worst parts?

4. What are some words to describe your ideal family culture?

5. What things would need to change for you to have this culture?

6. How are your children already contributing to your family culture?

7. What are you and your spouse contributing to your family culture?

Come Away from the Calendar

In the nineteenth century, families gathered around the hearth as the center of the home. It's where they came together for warmth, found comfort from the cold, and created lasting memories together. It's where they read books, made meals, shared a cup of cocoa, or reveled in rousing conversations.

But today, in place of the hearth, we have the calendar. Our lives are centered on activity, not community. A day at home is considered a day wasted. Boring at best, a failure at worst. Homes have become like charging stations where we eat, sleep, and change clothes before going out into the world, where our real lives are lived.

Society has duped us into believing that we have to do all the things other families are doing, in order to raise happy, healthy, whole adults: extracurricular activities, after-school sports, advanced-placement classes. These pressures prey upon our worries as parents that our kids will be left behind. We overthink, overreact, and overschedule their lives to counteract the feeling that we're going to fail them.

But all that activity isn't accomplishing what we think it is. The point of standing on the sidelines of a soccer field isn't to turn our eight-year-old into a star-athlete. It's to build a relationship.

If you don't feel like you're connecting with your kids, it's worth a look at your family culture. Are the decisions you are making *yours*? Are your kids thriving? Are you thriving as a family?

The solution to worrying isn't adding activity. It's removing the things that are causing you to be worried in the first place.

It's not about adding to-dos. It's about stripping away the excess and doing less to have a greater impact. You don't have to do all the things. Give yourself less to worry about.

So what should you include in your family culture? Any activity that builds relationship. It can include after-school programs, extracurricular activities, and travel-league sports. Or it can be nothing but hanging out together. We don't have to constantly be doing things in order to build relationship.

Time alone isn't the answer. It takes intentionality to create bonds with our children, more than just passing potatoes at the dinner table or rushing everyone into the car for a ballet rehearsal. Every moment, every activity, is an opportunity for connection and fostering family culture, but creating an intentional life may mean eliminating some things or adding others.

Let me be clear. There's nothing wrong with the activities and traditions of modern society. Most people enjoy them. A wonderful family culture can be forged in Friday night lights, swim meets, travel-league baseball, or Saturday morning soccer as much as it can in weekend camping trips, slow mornings, traveling the country, or living off the grid.

As long as it is intentional.

As long as it is life-giving.

As long as it is serving your family's purpose—and not the other way around.

There is no one right way of doing family. If what you're doing is working, then by all means keep doing it. That's the point, after all: carving your own wild path.

Our families may not have the same hobbies or pursue similar passions, but the culture of our homes isn't found in the kinds of activities we undertake. It's found in the relationships in which we have invested. Everything else is merely facade, like stone veneer laid over cheap plywood.

What more do you want for your family, and what are you willing to do to get it?

The Wild Path Less Traveled

Becoming a wild and free family is the difficult path, not the easy one. If you choose to put your family first . . . if you educate your children in a way that lets them pursue their own interests . . . if you believe that childhood is a time to be cherished and preserved, that it's not meant to be mere preparation for adulthood—you will be different. You will not be like everyone else.

And it's not always sustainable. We often abandon our family culture for short periods because of fatigue, work, and other pressures. It's like trying to hold a flexed muscle. Sometimes it feels good to let go every now and then. Just because we're not doing something all the time doesn't mean it's not a core value. There are some seasons when our family culture is stronger than others.

But coming together even once a week can set a pattern that will last the rest of our lives. For example, the things we remember about our childhoods didn't necessarily happen all the time. Many of them were merely moments, but they still constituted our family culture.

Whenever the world closes in around us, it fuels our family culture, rather than suffocates it. While the world rushes about doing, going, buying, and bustling, we embrace our family culture more than ever before. We worry less about what the world demands of us and more about making the most of this life in the ways of learning, crafting, reading, eating, and sipping (yes, we do a lot of the latter).

No one can tell you what your family culture should be.

That's up to you. But being a wild and free family means shaking off what matters to other people and following your own values and passions.

Most of us have only eighteen summers with our children at home. The time we have with our kids is limited, and this sobering reality ought to influence how we spend our time with those we love.

My friend Gabreial Wyatt has a teenage son who is a bit of a night owl. So, in order to spend more time with him, Gabreial and her husband often stay up late too. Whatever it takes.

Building a family culture from a foundation of relationships is risky business. It exposes our humanity and unravels our best intentions to achieve the pretty perception that everything is okay.

It is years of soul work in the trenches of daily trial and error. But we're not building a house in two weeks. We're laying the foundation for a fortress that will withstand the harshest winds and the fiercest storms. We are building an estate of love that will serve as a safe haven for years to come.

My dear friend Richele Baburina once described a conversation she overheard with a mother who clearly had a sense of her own family culture:

"Wouldn't you like to be a part of this?" someone asked.

"I'm sorry, I'm not available," the mother said.

"I understand. You're busy," the other person said.

"No," the mother responded. "I just don't want to *be* busy."

No one can tell you what your family culture should be. That's up to you. But being a wild and free family means shaking off what matters to other people and following your own values and passions.

Creating your own family culture starts with believing in the importance of preserving childhood for our kids, seeking to connect with them, understanding the unique ways they are wired, and creating a safe haven for them to learn, grow, and explore who they are. It's knowing there will be challenging seasons, that we all make mistakes, and that there's no perfect way to be a parent but that you are the perfect parent for your child. It's realizing that you can redeem the past, heal from generational traumas, and create a better future for your children.

When you choose to be wild and free instead of following society's conventions, you are not sabotaging your children's future. You are not limiting their options. You are not missing out.

You are restoring the very heart of your family.

2

TO PRESERVE CHILDHOOD

*When I became a man I put away
childish things, including the
fear of childishness and the desire
to be very grown up.*

—C. S. LEWIS

Yesterday afternoon, my seven-year-old was skipping past our foyer when she stopped and eyed a strange box sitting on the front stoop. In the age of Amazon deliveries for everything from rubber gloves to rotisserie chickens, our homelife is constantly being interrupted by the sound of the doorbell, followed by the incessant barking of our Pomeranian and the scamper of children running through the house in hopes that perhaps this delivery will, at long last, be for them.

Only this time, the doorbell hadn't rung.

"Mama," Annie called out. "There's a package at the door, and no one donged the dong-dong!"

The English major in me made a silent copy edit in my mind, but the mama in me didn't say a word. I simply smiled and jotted down my daughter's words in a notebook so I could cherish them forever.

Oh, to have those moments bottled up in a jar and saved to be repeated over and over again. Grammar lessons will come soon enough. The world will correct her missteps and call out her childlike wonder in time. But for now, our home is a sanctuary to her childhood. Her innocence is preserved here.

Childhood is meant to be a quiet, growing time, British educator Charlotte Mason wrote,[1] and yet it's been fast-tracked and fertilized to suit our modern standards of child development. We have so much fear that our children will fall behind that we end up correcting the childhood right out of them.

Joseph Chilton Pearce was a notable developmental psychologist and the author of *Magical Child*. He wrote, "We have a cultural notion that if children were not engineered, if we did not manipulate them, they would grow up as beasts in the field. This is the wildest fallacy in the world."[2]

We sacrifice their childhood on the altar of preparing them for adulthood.

But what if childhood *was* the preparation?

What if having a whole childhood *was* the key to a healthy adulthood?

Researcher and psychologist Peter Gray wrote, "We must give childhood back to children. Children must be allowed to follow their inborn drives to play and explore, so that they can grow into intellectually, socially, emotionally, and physically strong and resilient adults."[3]

Children Without Childhood

Everything that children naturally do—from making up games and catching bugs to climbing trees and spinning round and round on a swing until they're dizzy—plays a vital part in the development of their brains.

In essence, these experiences of childhood create a neurological blueprint for everything from how they will interact with the world to the way they think, feel, and learn.

We didn't know this, of course, when we started manufacturing experiences and putting progress and preparation over the protection and preservation of this formative time. No one wanted to destroy childhood at the expense of children themselves. But it happened, nonetheless.

In 1983, the *New York Times* published an article by Marie Winn titled "The Loss of Childhood," which described a cultural shift that had taken place in which childhood was being viewed as an age of preparation rather than an age of protection.[4]

As you can imagine, the consequences have been profound.

And this was before social media and smartphones.

Treating our children like adults has not only failed to make them more mature, but also hindered their ability to handle the pressures of adult responsibilities.

Winn wrote, "Perhaps an understanding that children and adults are not equal, and that children do not prosper when treated as equal, will encourage parents to take a more authoritative—authoritative, not authoritarian—position in the family."

Children, as it turns out, need a childhood.

They need time when they don't have to carry the burdens of their parents or have the pressures of adults. They need to know they can be carefree in this wild world.

The loss of childhood that was once an alarming trend thirty or forty years ago is now the norm.

"We are the kids who were 'so adult,'" one college student was quoted as saying in the article. "Our parents expected us to understand their problems and frustrations. . . . What we missed was the chance to be childish, immature, and unafraid to admit we didn't have it all together."[5]

When 90 percent of children between eight and sixteen have viewed pornography online,[6] and suicide is the second leading cause of death for fifteen-to-twenty-four-year-olds,[7] I think it's safe to say that our social experiment of expediting childhood has failed miserably.

Winn rightly concluded that "perhaps the recognition that a highly complicated civilization cannot afford to shorten the period of nurture and protection of its immature members will restore a real childhood to the children of coming generations."[8]

We may not be able to restore what's been lost for a previous generation, but we can make a difference for the children within our own homes. Preserving childhood starts in our own families.

Mother Teresa said if you want to change the world, go home and love your family.[9]

We must begin at home.

It All Begins at Home

I didn't mean to have my children spaced so far apart. Let's just say I was trying to savor each one.

Having five kids ranging in age from six to eighteen comes with its own set of dynamics, such as having built-in babysitters and feeling grandmotherly when I'm around mothers of preschoolers. But despite their age differences, my children's activities overlap in more ways than you might imagine.

It's not uncommon for me to walk into the kitchen in the morning and find all five of them huddled around the homemade playdough I set out the night before, going head-to-head in a game of memory-matching cards, or working together to construct a Lego set.

When the oldest ones see me coming, they quickly move on to something else. But it's too late. I have already delighted in seeing them embrace their childhood, if only for a moment.

When our children are young, they speak as children, understand as children, and think as children. And when they become adults, they're expected to put away childish things.

The trouble is that many children feel pressured to put away childish things long before it's time—all in the name of maturity.

Children are meant to be children, and studies show that burdening them with adult challenges is harmful to their emotional health. Parents may do this in the name of treating children as equals or perhaps leaning on their children for emotional support. But we are meant to be *their* emotional support, not the other way around.

Not only do children lose the security they need at home, but their brains aren't able to process deep emotions or difficult situations like a mature adult's brain. This "parentification" is not only harmful to their futures but also strips children of the freedom and joy of childhood.

Let's restore our homes as safe havens for our children, for their future's sake.

Filter the adult world. Fight to protect their innocence. Think twice before giving a child under eighteen a smartphone. Research the negative consequences of social media and pornography.

Reclaim your role as an adult, and let your children be children. Do the hard work of personal healing. Strive for emotional health. Fight for joy. Fight for love. Fight for home.

Create a haven of safety. Create a shelter of security. Create a home of peace.

The path to preserving childhood is a harrowing one. There are distractions at every turn and countless pressures looming on the other side of every wondrous landscape. But we can uphold a vision of what could be. There is nothing else that can give our children a childhood.

That, my friend, is something only you and I can do.

Let them climb, make mud pies, and splash in puddles.

Let them stretch their legs and lungs all at once.

Let them sing and shout and stand on their heads.

Let them discover new things in all different places.

Let them turn over logs and look for pollywogs.

Let them find all the worms for your new herb garden.

Let them learn new skills and make messes.

Let them make dandelion chains and learn to whistle with grass.

Let them skip rope and play hopscotch and call it a day.

Let them be happy, let them be whole.

Nourish them with healthy food, fresh air, and sunshine.

Don't just tell them, show them.

Go with them, go first, whatever it takes.

Do these things every single day.

We preserve childhood by seeking activities that slow down time, not hasten it. This doesn't mean abdicating our role as parents. It means accepting that *we* are our children's greatest experts. It means letting our kids become bored and being okay with it.

It's refusing to fall into the comparison trap.

It's facing our fears and failures and doing something about it.

It's trusting the innate desire to learn that's found in every child.

Recapture the Power of Relationships

"Mama, I don't want to grow up."

"Why not, my love?"

"Because I always want to be with you."

"I understand completely, sweetheart. I always want to be with you too."

"But I don't want to grow up."

"My darling, you are growing up so beautifully. You shine from the inside out. I love your lovely face, your adorable dimple, your bright eyes and beautiful smile. But you know what I love most about you?"

"My nose?"

I laugh.

"No. But it is perfect."

I kiss her nose.

"The thing I love most about you is your heart."

Her eyes grow big in a silly way. She laughs.

"Your heart is so full of love and life and joy and kindness. Your heart is going to change the world someday. And I can't wait to be there to watch. Oh darling, you don't ever have to worry. Growing up is not about leaving me, although you will probably want to do that someday too. Growing up is about becoming who you are meant to be. And I will always be here for you."

This bedtime conversation is just one of the many I've had with my precious littles over the past year. They come at it in different ways, but the point is the same: they relish our relationship.

A secure relationship is a place of safety, of peace, and of contentment.

Thinking about leaving that space feels scary and unsettling.

Throughout history, relationships have kept the world spinning.

There is a reason why poets, scribes, writers, and psychologists have proclaimed the power of relationships. Why people with strong relationships are 50 percent less likely to die prematurely. Why a lack of connection causes depression, increases blood pressure, and decreases immune function. And why solitary confinement is considered the cruelest of punishments.

Relationships are vital to our very existence.

But the importance of relationships isn't just a matter of the heart.

Trauma expert Bruce Perry said, "The human brain was not designed for the modern world."[10]

He was, of course, referring to modern culture, the way we live today as a society, including family constructs and technological advancements.

Perry continued, "For thousands of generations we lived in small, multi-generational groups. Children experienced more touch, more eye contact, more interaction. These things fed the brain in natural, rich ways. We've invented a world that is relationally different than the brain prefers."

The sad state of our current world is that "children have fewer emotional, social, and cognitive interactions with fewer people." We don't yet fully understand the impact of modern life on the developing child. We've lost the things that matter for families, as well as developmental growth. Things like family meals, talks around the fire, physical touch, and multigenerational relationships.

"We've created a poverty of relationships that is much worse than the poverty of material things," Perry said. This poverty makes it much more difficult for our children to learn new things, show empathy, respond to stress, and find meaningful connections with others.

But there is hope.

When we preserve childhood, we can recapture the power of relationships.

And though this modern world is doing everything it can to pull our families apart, we can find ways to create meaningful connections with our children, our families, and our communities.

Reclaim the Wonder of Childhood

The wonder of childhood is a curious thing. No one can define it, but we can recall what it was for us.

It is delight and awe, freedom and autonomy.

It is, as Wordsworth proclaimed, "the simple creed of childhood."

If we rush children through life, we prevent wonder. If we know all the answers, we hinder wonder. If we push children to perform, we stunt wonder. And if we constantly entertain our children, we extinguish wonder. We want to be protectors of wonder, not protectors *from* wonder.

To do this, we have to set aside our own adult notions of how to live. We must embrace the mindset of a child to remember what is necessary for them to grow and thrive.

Fresh air. Grass and dirt. Good books. Tickles and cuddles. Skipping and jumping. Healthy meals and hearty conversation. Being silly and acting their age. Making messes and getting dirty. Climbing trees. Building forts. Tears. Curiosity. Kindness. Dreams. Bravery. Laughter. Love.

With so many things fighting to strip wonder from our

children's hearts and minds, we cannot be complacent about preserving it. We must become wonder warriors.

Every day is a battle to keep wonder alive but also to reclaim it from all the ways it has been lost. And our children must see us as wonder allies, seeking out beauty and reveling in awe.

When my children beckon me outside to look at the massive Hunter's Moon because they know how much I love it—or when they come running inside from the backyard and shout, "Mom, we found the most beautiful flower! Do you want to come see it?"—I say yes and go, even when I'm making dinner, lest they think wonder is something you lose when you grow old and tired.

Reclaiming the wonder of childhood isn't fostering childish behavior but rather fostering *childlike* behavior, a posture of the heart that appears unjaded to the outside world, a state of mind that views imagination, delight, and wonder as the utmost of competencies.

When we give up on the fear of childishness, we can embrace the wonder of childhood.

And that is the beginning of everything.

3

TO CONNECT WITH YOUR KIDS

The hunger for love is much more difficult
to remove than the hunger for bread.

—MOTHER TERESA

'm no Mother Teresa. I hide in the bathroom and scroll through social media like any other mother who's had it up to her ears with the constant bickering or continual cries for "Mooooommm!" I've discovered the perfect volume at which to watch Instagram stories in my closet without being discovered.

But more than anything, I desire to connect with my kids.

"More than in any other human relationship—overwhelmingly more—motherhood means being instantly interruptible, responsive, responsible," wrote author Tillie Olsen.[1]

I make breakfast, switch the laundry, and empty the dishwasher, all in the middle of answering a simple text. The recipient will never know it took over an hour. I walk to the

bedroom in hopes of getting dressed but forget and end up folding a mountain of laundry, reading a book to my daughter, and listening to my son's latest song.

I published my first book at the age of forty and have written a half dozen more in my head in the shower over the past twelve years. There are books in me that will never be written because the important work of motherhood comes first. And if I'm honest, I wouldn't have it any other way.

I am not a saint, and I have my moments. But I know. I always know.

It's an honor to be my child's person.

It's a privilege to be called mother at all.

Everything I do feels like an Olympic feat because I am a mother of five, but I am everything I am because I have been a mother these past eighteen years.

I have learned—from working in the trenches, hiding in my bed on desperate days, and making more mistakes than any mother hopes to commit—that presence over perfection is what really matters.

Connection over Correction

When our children are uncooperative or misbehaving, it's not usually a discipline problem. It's a connection problem. Their actions express what their words cannot. They long to have a relationship with us, and when that connection is made, they are more teachable, more loving, more cooperative.

In her book *Connection Parenting*, Pam Leo wrote, "Our parenting effectiveness is in direct proportion to the strength of the connection we have with our child. When we have a strong connection, we don't have to resort to coercion."[2]

In Wild + Free, we use the phrase "connection before correction." But this isn't just a principle for home education. It's a principle for parenting. And while it sounds simple, it can be quite difficult.

It takes intention.

It takes practice.

It takes heart.

Our children don't know they need connection with us. They only know when something is missing. They have an unmet need, so they act out, respond badly, or misbehave in an effort to engage with us.

They offer an unspoken invitation for us to connect with them, but because it comes disguised as stinging words, temper tantrums, and emotional outbursts, we see it as a problem to solve rather than an opportunity to draw near. When we respond badly in turn, we only widen the chasm even more, confirming their worst fears: that they aren't loved, safe, accepted, or understood.

By sending our children away, we tell them they don't belong.

By addressing only their outward behavior, we ignore their hearts.

By shouting at them, we cause their bodies and brains to go into fight-or-flight mode. Their cortisol levels rise, making it even more difficult for them to respond in the way we desire.

To be a parent is to be part nurturer, part negotiator. If we're not careful, the tactics we use to "solve the problem" can make the situation more frustrating or even confusing.

I have a friend who called her ten-year-old son's bluff to run away from home at ten o'clock one night. She told him to dress warmly and let him march right out the front door, thinking he would change his mind once he got to the end of the sidewalk.

Instead, when he didn't answer her calls, she frantically searched the neighborhood in her car, but to no avail. A stranger called an hour later to say that he had found him. My friend never dreamed it would go that far. She never imagined their relationship would become so fractured. She was horrified at the thought of what could have happened to her child.

Doing right by our kids is hard. It's even harder when our to-do list is miles long and our fuses are short. It's even more challenging when we ourselves suffer from disconnection, an empty cup, and all the other pressures that come with life.

It's doubly hard when our children, by the sheer nature of their personalities and wills, challenge the simple guidelines of our homes throughout the day.

As adults, most of life doesn't go our way. That's a given. People in authority bark orders at us all day long. We get rejected and refused by those who have the power to help us. Plans fall through.

Our home is the one place where we have a say.

But not for long.

Introduce kids. Their wide-eyed, bed-headed, food-stained faces staring up at us, longing to know and be known, craving to hear and be heard, desiring to see and be seen.

But all we can think about is how we're going to pay the bills, who's going to walk the dog, why our insurance costs went up, when we're getting our tax refund, and what we're making for dinner.

And that doesn't even touch on our internal worlds.

We have so much to deal with. Don't our kids know what's expected of them?

Can't they help make our lives easier?

If only they would listen.

If only they wouldn't argue.

If only they wouldn't talk back to us.

If only they would do as they're told.

But these precious souls only know their father or mother and the innate desire to be loved by them. How can we blame them if they haven't learned how to articulate their needs?

Love is made manifest in such a way that we, being their parents, do not consider our authority as adults to be used for our own advantage. Rather, we put ourselves on their level, humble ourselves, connect with them, and make ourselves available to be their companions, playmates, and friends.

Children have enough authorities in their lives. That's all most adults are to them.

Kids don't need parents who are skilled in correcting them.

They need parents who are willing to connect with them.

Three Steps to Connection

There is no shortcut to connection. When it comes to raising children and helping them overcome challenges, there is no easy route. There is only the long road. There is only the hard way through.

Pam Leo wrote that when our children's connection tanks get low, they communicate their needs through behavior: "The level of cooperation parents get from children is usually equal to the level of connection children feel with their parents."[3]

None the wiser, we react to the symptoms, rather than the root cause, and use our parental authority to set things right. We've all been there. There are words. There are tears. And there is complete and utter exhaustion at the end of a long, drawn-out process to restore order in the home.

It's easier to react to the symptoms of our children's

The Friendship of Family

When I think about family, the word that often comes to mind is "friendship." Some would say that you can't be both a parent and a friend to your children. But I disagree.

Think about what friends do. They laugh and love together, hurt and forgive each other. They eat meals together, share life, and make time for each other. They speak truth when necessary but more often embolden and encourage each other. True friends become family.

So why can't our family be friends?

As I write these words, my mind is flooded with all the ways I misuse my parenting-friendship with my children. I think about the times when I'm tired, stressed, hangry, or just plain exasperated. Too often, in these moments, I abandon my role as a loving friend and resort to my authority as a parent. It's easier to give quick commands than tend to their hearts and minds amid challenging circumstances.

But I will never stop striving to be the close friend my children need, the friend who believes in them, endures with them, and helps them become the best version of themselves.

Psychologist Jean Piaget wrote, "How much more precious is a little humanity than all the rules in the world."[4]

I want to love my children, to be slow to anger and quick to forgive. I want to hold space for them and to hold them. I want to look past their outward behavior and see their hearts. And I want to speak truth but show support for them at all times.

The ways we engage.

The words we choose.

How we treat each other.

They all matter.

Parenting sage and esteemed author Sally Clarkson said, "Love is the most profound tool of influence in the lives of your children."[5]

Having a friendship with our kids is not a given simply because we gave birth to them. It's a practice that comes from taking advantage of small opportunities, much like we do with our adult friends.

It's singing along to their favorite song on the car radio. It's sitting on the floor and playing a board game. It's making their favorite meal or tucking a note into their backpack. It's showing up with a kind word, a gentle hug, or a conversation about their latest adventure in Minecraft.

It's leaving a lipstick letter on their bathroom mirror.

Extraordinary lives are created in the community of family. Character is birthed in the chaos of relationships. Beautiful hearts are grown in the garden of a relationship-rich childhood.

And friendship with our children is where it all begins.

emotional needs. After all, we can see them playing out in front of us. There is nothing to decipher about a tantrum, no hidden message to uncover with an outburst. But it comes at the expense of connection, which would have taken the same amount of time on the front end, preserved our energy, and left our children's spirits intact.

The choice is ours.

"Either we spend time meeting children's emotional needs by filling their cup with love, or we spend time dealing with behaviors caused from their unmet needs," Leo wrote. "Either way, we spend time."[6]

Parenting is a privilege. Our children are worthy of our honor and respect. And taking time to walk through the steps of connection is the best way to nurture them through difficulty.

There are three steps to follow: calm them, connect with them, and communicate with them.

STEP 1: CALM THEM

I have a child with an overactive amygdala, which is the almond-shaped mass of gray matter inside the cerebral hemisphere of the brain that is responsible for big emotions, such as fear, anger, and trust.

It is widely accepted among scientists and researchers that the amygdala is also responsible for the instincts of fight or flight, the survival response within each of us.

We've been doing cognitive therapy with him for several years and are seeing tremendous improvements, but for years, he was constantly on the lookout for dangers and threats.

One night several years ago, long after the kids were asleep, Ben and I were making popcorn on the stove in preparation for watching a movie. I left the kernels on the burner a little too long, and the smoke detector went off. Within a minute, my son came flying out of the back bedroom and ran right out the front door. After a few seconds, he came back inside and announced that it was okay: the roof was *not* on fire.

Ben and I were still standing there in our pajamas.

This is the same child who becomes frantic when our six-year-old strays too far from us in public or when my husband pulls into a (restricted) handicap parking space to wait for me at the grocery store.

It's nice to have a personal security officer in the family, but there is also a downside. When my son is triggered by something or when he goes into fight-or-flight mode, there is no way to rationalize with him. He has to work through all those big emotions of fear, worry, anger, and distrust.

It's easier to handle when it comes to things like burnt popcorn, but it's much more difficult to navigate when he's acting irrationally toward us or his siblings. When this happens, I can't do anything to stop it. Trust me, I've tried. But after years of trial and error, I know that all I can do is wait it out and talk with him when he's ready.

One time, that meant sitting on the bathroom floor for thirty minutes until he made it through a complete cycle of emotions. By allowing him to work through these feelings in my presence, I let him know that he and his emotions are safe with me. That he has nothing to fear. I'm not going anywhere.

We've made huge strides together, and it's never been difficult to love him. But it has been one of the greatest challenges of my life to walk through this with him. To love him in a way that he feels it. To show patience in the midst of frustration. And to hold space for his behavior without judgment.

He has thrown objects, broken furniture, slammed doors, and said horrible things. But over time, I have grown into the kind of mother who makes sure he knows that his big emotions are safe with me. Once he realizes he's safe, he returns to the compassionate, loving, and tender child I know him to be.

And today, as the connections in his brain are growing as strong as his connection with us, he doesn't need to throw things or have outbursts in order to express words or feelings

I love the principle that Pam Leo proposes for parents, called "Rewind, Repair, Replay." The process looks like this:

1. Rewind—acknowledge our hurtful behavior ("What I said was hurtful")

2. Repair—apologize and let the child know he did not deserve our response

3. Replay—respond to your child with love and listen to them[7]

that he can't manage in any other way. He has found his voice. He can express the frustration but is able to process and regulate his emotions in a healthy way.

This might be an extreme example for your family, but the same principle applies.

All children need connection. But as parents quickly discover, they aren't always open to it. Before we can connect with our kids, we have to calm them, which looks different for each child. Connection isn't possible when our kids are upset or in the middle of an emotional cycle they can't escape.

Being able to regulate emotions, for both parents and children, is vital to maintaining a calm household. But as any parent knows, some days are harder than others. Whether it's waking up on the wrong side of the bed, getting hangry, contending with the "witching hour" at four o'clock, or straining against the moon's gravitational pull on the Earth, some days we don't stand a chance.

What we need is a protocol for proceeding peacefully—like "stop, drop, and roll" to put out the fire or like a map to the exits or an escape hatch for the reactions that cause even more harm in our relationships.

"Sometimes a child's behavior will push our buttons and we react rather than respond," Pam Leo wrote, which isn't the best way to handle their behavior.[8] It often exacerbates the situation. By us asking our kids to rewind, repair, and replay their response instead, we effectively give them a do-over.

What a grace-filled approach to correcting behaviors. All of us need second chances.

Sometimes the calming phase takes longer than we'd like. Adults as well as children need time to cool off, walk it off, or shake it off. This can take minutes or even hours. We can't rush it.

Calming a child can look like a big hug, simply sitting with them, or giving them space to be alone. Calming can even look like climbing a tree, taking a bath, or building a Lego creation. Regardless of what calming looks like for your child, it must happen before real connection can take place.

It takes a lot of restraint to say, "I don't have to parent or discipline this behavior out of my child right now. I can give them space to calm down so we can talk about it."

STEP 2: CONNECT WITH THEM

Every spring, I begin working on the garden boxes in my backyard. I either build new ones or repair the old ones that have been battered by the cold winters of the Virginia coast, where snow dissipates into freezing rain. I position the boxes in just the right place for sunlight and then fill them with dirt.

This act of preparation requires vision. Plotting where the tomatoes and strawberries will get the most sun. Deciding which flowers will look nice along the house. And selecting the plants for in front of the garden shed. In my mind's eye, I can see how things will look when the flowers reach their majestic fullness by midsummer.

When everything is in position, when all is set right, then it is time to plant the seeds.

The same is true of our families. Only when our children are calm can we truly connect with them. Only then can we plant the seeds. They take root because the soil is receptive. This can be as simple as a conversation, a game of UNO, or a meal together. You know your children best.

Our days are made by the small acts of love we commit and the intentional moments we create. They are formed in the way we see our children in the morning light and the prayers we whisper over their beds at night. The smiles and stories and sweet treats we offer. The hard days and bad calls and long cries in the closet. It all adds up in the grand narrative of our life together as a family.

There are, of course, the big ways we intentionally connect with our kids. Family trips. Whole days together, just for them—as a tribe or one-on-one. When we plan a special event or set aside a time to spend with each child, they feel valued. When they know we have made them a priority, they feel loved. When we focus on just them with no distractions, they feel cherished.

But the everyday, in-between moments are equally important. The brief shoulder rub at the dinner table, the small token "that made me think of you," or the kind word when you pass in the hallway. It's amazing how these little gestures transform our children.

And then there is play.

For a child, play is the language of connection.

There is no "working together" to build a relationship. No

"parental pep talk" to forge a bond. No filling of a child's cup merely through close proximity.

According to author and counselor Vince Gowmon, play is "the language of a child's soul."[9] Any other expression of love might look familiar, but it's not their native tongue.

Once, when my husband was traveling to Quebec for a conference, he arrived at the Montreal International Airport fully prepared to encounter their French-speaking population. The customs agent asked for his passport, and without thinking, Ben said, "I'm sorry, I speak English."

The offended agent looked at him and cried out, "So do I!"

We have the capability to speak our children's language—if only we would listen.

We may not remember everything our parents did with us as children, but all of us remember when they played with us. I don't mean the kind of play where children are invited to join *our* endeavors. We can all tolerate our own version of play. A backyard game of Frisbee to show off the skills we honed in college. Watching the big game without speaking. Teaching our children how to play Jenga *the right way*.

There's a temptation to substitute activities that look like play and smell like play but have nothing to do with play at all. Only play is memorable. Children will not be deceived by counterfeits.

I'm talking about the kind of play where we join *their* endeavors. There is nothing more thrilling to a child than for a parent to stop the Earth from spinning and crouch down at their level to play. I only need to enter my children's bedrooms and join in their play for it to feel like Christmas morning to them.

Every day, my two little girls, Annie and Millie, beg me to stop working, put down my laptop, or whatever I happen to be doing, and embody one of the Lego characters they have assigned to me. (It's usually a strange-looking lizard or a pizza delivery guy with the facial features rubbed off.) I use my best lizard voice or delivery driver impression until they stop me in my tracks and correct me.

"A lizard would never talk like that, Mom!"

I make the required vocal adjustments and do my best improvising to move the plot forward until, once again, they correct my version of things and set me back on the right course.

It's at times like these when I have to remind myself that my girls have not invited me to play. They have invited me to connect. And by playing, I'm connecting with them in the best way they know how.

May I never grow tired of speaking like a lizard, lest they stop wanting to connect with me at all.

"We will always know when connection is re-established," Pam Leo wrote. "When children feel connected, they make eye contact with us, they talk to us, and they welcome our touch."[10]

Strengthening the connection with our children is a lot like strengthening a muscle. It takes consistent action, over time, and cannot be achieved in a day. The weaker the connection is, the longer it will take to see results. And the more often you use it, the stronger the connection becomes.

The beautiful part about connecting with our children is that it opens their hearts to let us guide them, direct them, and become the parents we were always meant to be.

STEP 3: COMMUNICATE WITH THEM

When our children are calm and connected, we have the opportunity to communicate with them. Then and only then can we revisit the issue that started the whole mess and lead our children through it.

The communication stage is for teaching, nurturing, and guiding our children.

It's when we can address the issue, talk to them about their behavior, or ask them to share what they're thinking and feeling. It's when we can communicate harder and bigger things than a disconnected relationship allows. It's what we really wanted to say in the first place.

Only this time, they welcome it. Their hearts are open and ready to receive what we have to say.

They'll look us in the eyes. Respond to our words. Let us touch them. They'll give us a smile and open their hearts. And we'll know if we've really connected, Pam Leo said, if they dance with us.

It is connection that provides the foundation for these teaching moments. It is the same issue we tried to address in the first place, but this time, the child is open to hearing us. They still may not like what we have to say, but they're receptive. A connected child is a cooperative child.

Keep in mind that less is more when it comes to our words. Communication is mostly about listening. For everything you say, remember to ask questions.

One of my favorite questions is "What is it that you heard me say?" because often what we intend to say isn't what they hear. This allows us to clarify what we are communicating and ultimately leads to healthier and more effective exchanges.

Maybe they didn't mess up. Maybe *we* messed up. It was our curt reaction that caused the hurt feelings. We all have the potential to behave badly, to act immaturely, to hurt other people. But just because there was a disconnection doesn't mean they're off the hook. Whether it is mouthing off or not doing their chores or throwing something on the floor and refusing to pick it up, we need to talk about it. But we look for a time when they are feeling connected to address the issue.

Alfie Kohn, the author of *Unconditional Parenting*, wrote that it's not how *we* feel about our kids, but about how they *think* we feel about them.[11] Our children should never feel like we merely want them to behave. They should feel like our relationship comes first, that we love and care for them.

Let's face it. Even on our best days, we mess up with our kids. We use a harsh tone, we don't meet them at their level, we neglect to connect with them, or we just plain behave poorly. And we almost always know when our actions or reactions have caused disconnection. They know it and eventually we know it.

The Creed of Connection

Today I will make my home a haven for my children with kind words and gentle answers.

Today I will listen to their needs and remember they aren't always expressed with words.

Today I will talk less and notice more.

Today I will be their calm in the midst of chaos.

Today I will read a book aloud or help them with their math but remember that my greatest role is to love them.

Today I will do a thousand little things that go unnoticed but notice when they make a difference.

Today I won't let the fear of failure stop me from trying something new.

Today I will simply begin again.

Yet for some reason, it's far easier to fly off the handle and respond in kind.

The other day, I was stopped short by an Instagram post by a regretful mother of grown children who confessed that she had wished their early years would pass more quickly: the sleepless nights, the temper tantrums, the rebellious teenagers. Now she spends her days longing for her children to come home.

May we savor each godforsaken day of parenthood.

May we bless every Lego block we encounter underfoot.

And may we filter out the barbs of their rebellion to hear their heartfelt pleas.

I've learned so much from my children this week. They've shared some important concerns with me, a soapbox of thoughts, if I'm honest. And it's not that they didn't need to hear what I had to say, but it was equally important that I heard them too. They shared their needs, and I listened. Their words took my breath away and sank deep into my soul. They showed me how to be a better mother.

Even in the midst of frustration, I could hear their hearts.

Oh, may I always be so willing to listen.

I'm thankful that children's spirits are resilient, that mercies are made new every morning. And I cringe at having to need frequent reminders of my own values and passions. But I do. We all do.

A few things I was reminded of this week: Our teens need our tenderness just as much as our toddlers, if not more. And our little ones aren't too little to be included in our big plans.

Our children are not and never will be cogs in a system, family or otherwise. They are intelligent, thoughtful individuals who need both our vision and their own voice. They are wise beyond their years, all the while graced with childlike innocence. And I'm honored to grow and learn alongside these beautiful souls.

Stay Up for Them

My friend Betsy Jenkins wrote this lovely piece on connecting with teenagers, which she kindly allowed me to include here:

One thing I've learned after twenty years of parenting is that it doesn't necessarily get easier, but it does change. As I parent my two teens and launch one young adult, I've found that they need me to be present for them, just as much as my toddlers did. They need my mind and heart engaged.

While a toddler needs cuddles, play, and physical help from us, our teens need a sounding board, a cheerleader, and, far less often than I find myself giving it, our experience and wisdom.

Often, I see parents facing their teens' desire for independence by either clamping down and trying to control them or by releasing them to flounder. In the simple phrase "stay up for them," I am trying to convey a philosophy for parenting teens and young adults.

Stay up for them when they come in from a night out. Stay engaged even when you have other work to do. Sacrifice your downtime when they need to pour out their hearts or just feel connected.

It used to be that my parenting work ended at 8:00 p.m., at least until the first nighttime feeding. My husband and I would have our alone time. Now, we usually have at least two boys up until we go to bed. But that time we spend with our teens in the evening has become one of my favorite parts of the day.

They really are such fun, cool, and interesting people. I am so glad that I chose to alter my expectations

when it came to our evenings. I would have missed out on so much joy and connection had I insisted on maintaining my downtime. I have the great honor of being their safe place to land during this season of growth and change.

As they tentatively take steps out into the world, they can come back to me to remind them who they are and encourage them. I love having teens. It is like the sweet, sweet reward for years of habit training and mess cleaning. They still have their moments. But that's it. They're just moments. Connect with your kids' hearts today. You will reap a harvest of friendship if you do not give up.[12]

My kids aren't taking any advanced-placement courses or starring in any upcoming productions. They aren't running for class president or winning any sports championships. But they are growing beautifully. Blooming at their own pace. Discovering who they are and learning to express themselves. And shining their light as best they can.

And their mother is growing in grace too.

May we always seek connection over correction.

It's Never Too Late

Somewhere in the midst of changing diapers, running a business, and adding new children to our homeschool rhythm, my eldest son became a teenager.

He's always been an old soul of sorts, either burying his nose in a book or jotting down ideas to write his own. He quickly went from turning pages to scrolling screens, as his new laptop became a prevalent part of his day—both with personal pursuits and certain school subjects.

As an introverted kid, he's always kept to himself, and our house is a bit of a barracks for seven people, with very few places to be alone. But after repeated attempts to start a conversation, invite him on outings, or spend quality time with him, just him and me, I finally came to the agonizing realization that he just didn't want to engage very much with me anymore.

One-word answers. Shoulder shrugs. Passes to participate.

He's a teenager, I thought. *Give him time.*

But weeks became months, and the months became—what seemed like—a lifetime of disconnection with my darling boy. My gut told me it didn't have to do with him being fifteen as much as it had to do with him and me. I can still feel the lump in my throat as I wondered if I had missed my opportunity.

Something happens when your boy becomes a teenager. You start counting down the days until they leave the house—and not in a good way. Every holiday seems like one of the last you'll have under the same roof. Every meal feels like one of the last you'll share together.

And when your young man stops engaging in familiar ways, whether due to his age or interests, it makes the time all the more fleeting.

After some deep soul-searching, I resolved to try again, no matter how long it took. But days of failed attempts turned into months of repeatedly missing the mark, and then I gave up completely.

Clarity came when I formally retired from parenting altogether on a cold December night. I've since rejoined the ranks in case you're wondering, but on this particular evening, I surrendered my role in a puddle of tears and despair. I didn't know what I had done but feared that I had ruined the relationship.

"It's just too hard," I told Ben. "I've lost his affections, and I'll never get them back."

I cried. Ben encouraged me. But the question remained: How do I reconnect with this kid?

I kept going.

I kept looking for open windows.

I kept turning the key in the lock.

And one day, I heard the first click.

I can't remember what I was cooking, but he came out to the kitchen and mentioned something he had been reading, something I knew very little about. But I kept to the task of stirring and gave him all the murmurs of intrigue and approval I could muster. As he continued sharing, his eyes came alive with excitement, regaling me with all the ins and outs of this particular fascination.

I leaned in, listened, and went along for the ride.

I managed to ask a few pseudo-intelligent questions about the topic, which kept him going. And I found myself experiencing the same bond we used to share when he was a little boy, both of us sitting on top of the slide at the park, eating almonds and throwing them to the squirrels.

It was a fleeting moment, like a shooting star streaking across the sky. It made me want to stand up and shout, "There it is! What a marvelous thing!" But I dared not show excitement for fear of scaring him off. As he left the kitchen, leaving me to finish cooking dinner alone, the smile wouldn't leave my face. And I've never stopped looking for shooting stars each and every day.

It's been a few years since that day, and despite the occasional disturbance in the force, we have found the delightful ease in our relationship again. In truth, he is one of my best friends.

When mothers ask me if it's too late for their older children, my answer is never.

And it's never too late to undo any damage you feel you may have caused.

Here's the thing: we're going to mess up because that's a part of life. Maybe you've made catastrophic mess-ups. It's not too late to repair those either. The beautiful thing about human nature is that we all crave restoration, even—or most especially—with those who have hurt us the most.

My children. Your children. They all desire to be restored to us. Connected with us.

It may not come easily or quickly, but all it takes is one day.

One meal. One hug. One book read aloud.

One cry. One laugh. One walk around the block.

One question. One problem. Curious and curiouser.

One smile. One game. One meaningful conversation.

Just one day.

A Benediction

As a mama of five wildly different individuals, I long to provide the connection each of them needs to fill their cups and keep them feeling loved and part of this big, beautiful, imperfect family of ours.

But each day, I fall short. I fail to fulfill my desire to connect on their level, play their favorite game, or engage patiently with their antics. I fail to respond lovingly, and I behave badly at times.

Having the right tools doesn't mean I always use them correctly. Just as I use the back of a screwdriver for a hammer when I'm too lazy to get the toolbox, sometimes I grab the nearest emotional tool in my belt. Frustration. Anger. Mean words. When that happens, I confess to behaving badly. I ask for forgiveness. But I cannot immediately ask for anything in return. Connection must happen first.

I remind myself that I'm a work in progress, and I am learning to give myself grace and not throw in the towel. Most importantly, I try to remember that I'm not alone.

You don't have the only child who misbehaves. You aren't the only parent walking through this right now. Whether your child is especially difficult, all kids misbehave. All kids react badly at certain times. And all kids respond to connection over correction.

Don't give up.

Don't get so discouraged with the lack of progress that you think it's not worth trying. I promise you it is always worth it. Anything worth doing is always going to be difficult.

There is a sweet promise written in the book of ages that those who trust will renew their strength. They will soar on wings like an eagle. They will run and not grow weary. They will walk and not be faint.[13] You can make it through this moment, this season. And you are growing beautifully.

I'm rooting for you today. May there be sweet moments of connection with your kids, sparks of wonder to engage their minds, and amazing grace to cover inevitable mishaps.

This journey is far from perfect, but it sure is beautiful.

Let love guide you.

With your kids, with others, and with yourself.

TO UNDERSTAND
YOUR CHILDREN

*Talk with your children and you will
hear their voice. Walk with them through
life and you will feel their heart.*

—GEOFF REESE

C hildren don't grow up seeing themselves as part of a herd. They may have brothers and sisters and, yes, sometimes lots of them, but kids only know themselves and the personal relationships they have with their parents. And yet it's easier to raise them as a group, to corral them together.

If one kid plays sports, they're all playing sports because of schedules and carpooling. If one of them wants Chipotle, they're all eating Chipotle because we're not going to more than one restaurant. A bookworm in a family of athletes is an aberration. A quiet kid in an extroverted family is an outlier. And a child who would rather travel the world than go to college can turn his parents' world upside down.

But the greatest gift we can give our children is to understand them. Individual attention takes time and effort. Oh, so much effort. Our children can be so unlike us.

Sometimes my eldest child will stand beside me in the kitchen while I'm baking bread or fixing dinner and talk at length about investment strategies or business opportunities, and I have had to google things after we spoke so I could better engage with him the next time.

My middle child will text me funny memes, favorite quotes, links to his latest podcast, or pictures with his head photoshopped onto famous people's bodies. He loves a good joke, a word of encouragement, random facts, and text messages that include an abundance of emojis and punctuation marks.

My youngest daughter is a snuggler. She begins each day in our bed getting a full body hug—legs interlocked, cheeks touching—topped off with a smothering of kisses. And if she slinks out of bed before me, she always lets me know that she'll be back in a few minutes for another snuggle.

These conversations and behaviors are reflections of their personalities, true, but they are also the cries of their hearts. And if I listen closely, I can get a glimpse at their longings, their dreams, their very souls. All these small things speak to who they are.

Kids long to feel seen and known. Thankfully, we have an abundance of tools at our disposal: the Myers-Briggs Type Indicator (MBTI), StrengthsFinder, the five love languages, archetypes, and the Enneagram, among many others. We have to be careful not to label our children and instead allow them to experiment and try on various preferences as they grow older. After all, the greatest tool in our relationship belt is the desire to listen, study, and spend time with our children. But these other tools can be a valuable resource for helping us understand and affirm them with specific words and helpful means of interaction.

My father happens to be an expert in the MBTI. He once came to visit my sister and me when our boys were performing in a children's choir. As he watched them singing onstage, he leaned over and whispered their personality types to us, merely from observation. One of them was joyfully involved in the performance without attempting to replicate the exact motions to the song. One of them hardly participated at all, with no sense of obligation to follow along. And the other concentrated hard on the teacher, trying to mimic her every move, in order to get the performance exactly right. We delighted in seeing their unique personalities onstage and chuckled at how different they were.

When we group our kids into the same "herd" with no regard for their personal preferences, we miss out on the unique expressions and personalities they bring to our families. And we misunderstand or even demonize kids who don't come at the world in the same way we do.

"Why weren't you participating?" we could have asked our middle child. Or "next time, loosen up and you'll enjoy it more," we could've told our oldest.

But conforming is not the point. Being *uniquely you* is something we accept and encourage in our household.

We have some good friends who were troubled by their teenage son, who came home from high school each day and locked himself in his room for hours before finally coming out for dinner. They wondered if he was being bullied or was hiding a dark secret. They longed for him to come out and talk, but he said he was fine. As they shared this story with me, a fellow introvert, a light bulb went off.

"He might just be restoring his energy," I suggested. "He's been expending it all day and desperately needs to recharge."

These two extroverted friends of mine looked at each other and then back at me.

"We need you to remind us of that often," the mother said.

Some kids are born into households with completely different family environments and can feel like they must have been switched at birth.

My sister Tiffany, for example, was born into a family very much unlike her personality type. She always felt loved and accepted while growing up, but because the rest of us are such abstract thinkers, she never felt like her family was "her people."

My parents were well versed in personality types, so they saw Tiffany's strengths and affirmed them, but she needed an outlet with others who were more like her. She found this through friends at school, her volleyball team, and a best friend who lived nearby.

Despite our different tendencies, we are dear friends today, as well as close sisters. She went on to become a successful chiropractor and business owner, and she keeps our family connected with her unique strengths and personality.

Understanding our children takes time and intentionality. It takes doing what *you* like some of the time and doing what *they* like the rest of the time. And it requires getting to know them over and over again through each stage of their development.

The work of understanding our children is never finished. We might think we understand them only to discover that we are lost again. We wonder what happened. How did we get it all wrong?

But the work of knowing never stops. Our children aren't growing just physically but also mentally, emotionally, and spiritually. They are constantly trying on different ideas, personas, and characteristics.

Harry Truman once said, "I have found the best way to give advice to your children is to find out what they want and then advise them to do it."[1]

Our job is not to judge but to join their journey of discovery.

Why Understanding Our Kids Is Hard

Understanding our children isn't as easy as it sounds. Sure, we can "type" them. We can apply labels to how they learn or behave. We can observe them in their natural habitat to see what lights them up. But there are barriers to understanding our children, including behavioral issues, learning challenges, and other struggles. These things get in the way of seeing who they truly are.

But what if the barriers aren't in our children, but in us? What if, in intuiting our way through parenting, we have guessed wrong in certain areas? What if the obstacle to understanding our children doesn't lie in their ambiguity, but in our inability to make sense of their seemingly incongruent behavior?

For decades, there have been parenting books claiming to teach the right way to raise children, magazine articles on dealing with tantrums, and programs designed to bring up children in the way they should go. There is an entire industry providing curricula, school programs, and reading regimens all crafted to help our children learn better, behave better, and become respectable members of society.

The trouble is, they aren't working.

As parents, we are given the highest charge of raising a human being, a tiny person to honor and respect, and showing them how to live in this big, wide world. Most parents want the very best for their children, but few of us know exactly what that is in all areas.

In their captivating book *NurtureShock*, Po Bronson and Ashley Merryman reveal why our parental instincts are so off the mark at times. What we think are "instincts" are often just "intelligent, informed reactions" based on "wishful thinking, moralistic biases, contagious fads, personal history, and old (disproven) psychology—all at the expense of common sense."[2]

For example, despite what self-help parenting books try to teach us, studies show that trying to encourage our children by telling them they're smart actually has the opposite effect.

Perhaps our job as mothers and fathers isn't to have these beautiful changelings all figured out, but to continually try to understand them as they morph and grow. To recognize that we don't know all the answers but to keep looking all the same. To accept that kids are walking contradictions at times because that is how they figure out life. To see that their comfort with duality is discomforting only to us because we want so desperately to understand them. And to acknowledge that our efforts to understand them aren't in vain but will sometimes fall short, nonetheless.

We are going to get things wrong when it comes to understanding our kids. Sometimes, we'll miss the mark so profoundly that we'll wonder if we should have ever become parents in the first place.

Today, there are all kinds of parents and even more parenting styles. Merriam-Webster's dictionary even lists several types of parents based on animals and machines:[3]

Helicopter parents who hover over their children to keep them safe

Snowplow parents who remove all obstacles from their children's path, from getting them switched to a gifted class to calling the coach to make sure they get to play

Tiger parents who believe in tough love and set high goals for their children's success and behavior

Jellyfish parents who have a few loose rules and tend to be overly permissive

And, of course, **free-range parents** who want to build resiliency in their children by giving them more freedom to explore the world and make decisions

To be honest, I don't care what we call this thing. But I do hope we can begin to see the factors that influence our perceptions. It starts with asking ourselves whether we are projecting our own childhood blisses and blunders onto our children or relying on old, disproven psychological theories we read in a book with biased research.

Sifting our wishful thinking from the reality, like chaff from the wheat, is a process. But as we begin to dismantle the artificial facade that has been plastered over our role as parents, I hope we'll see that raising children is less of what we do and more of who we are.

Validating Your Child's Experience

Our children seek validation in who we are, from every smile, every glance, every interaction of the day. From the newborn babe with sweet, milk-stained cheeks to the scruffy-faced teen towering over us, they all need our validation.

They need our faces to reflect our hearts for them. They need our actions to match our words to them. They need our emotions to hold enough strength for theirs. They need our truth to hold enough space for theirs. They need to know we are there for them. They need us to listen.

Enter in our human state. Our flawed existence. Our failures in number.

There is no formula for parenting. No step-by-step process for securing our child's heart. No "easy button" we can press to meet their needs. But still we try.

I, for one, am chief of sinners. I pronounce my values while confronting my inadequacies daily. Just the other day, I was in the kitchen prepping dinner, cleaning up messes, and chatting with my favorite child (wink wink, Dylan). He was extra boisterous and said a number of things to push my buttons in jest, but my capacity was full. After listening to his thoughts and feelings about my cooking, his course work for co-op, and various people in the house, I shut him down. I sent him away, and he stormed out.

Later, when we had a chance to talk a little more calmly about what happened, I gave him a wonderful speech full of amazing points that I thought ended the argument. When I was done, he said, "Okay. Now can I say something? Because you haven't listened to me once through this whole thing."

Ouch. He was right.

The fact is, I hadn't wanted to listen to him because I was convinced he had nothing to say that could change my perspective on the situation. But that isn't the point of listening. The point of listening is to seek understanding and let the other person know they are heard and valued.

The author Laurie Buchanan said, "When we listen, we hear someone into existence."[4]

Nonverbal communication is just as powerful as our words. We do this by affirming others with our facial expressions and reactions while they're speaking. And after they're finished, it's helpful to repeat back to them what they said as a way to let them know they've been heard.

No need to complicate it.

Talk with your children.

Listen to them.

When they tell you who they are, believe them. When they tell you something different the next day, believe them then too. They are ever-growing, ever-changing, and ever-becoming their beautiful selves—one day and one messy moment at a time.

Recognizing Your Child's Genius

Most kids are made to think there is only one kind of intelligence: the test-taking kind, the kind that scores high on quizzes, spelling bees, standardized tests, or the SATs. And this perception shapes their view of themselves for most of their lives, diminishing their dreams and reducing their confidence.

But if any breakthrough has occurred in the twenty-first century—where education is no longer viewed as a product of the industrial age, with students being churned out like widgets on an assembly line, but rather a cultivation of each child's aptitudes—it's that there is more than one type of intelligence.

In his book *Awakening Genius in the Classroom*, Thomas Armstrong described several of them:[5]

- **Logical-Mathematical Intelligence:** gifted in computer programming, math, and science

- **Spatial Intelligence:** gifted in art, invention, and design

- **Bodily-Kinesthetic Intelligence:** gifted at sports, dance, acting, and hands-on learning

- **Musical Intelligence:** gifted at singing, songwriting, rapping, or playing instruments

- **Interpersonal Intelligence:** gifted at leading, social direction, and being a sympathetic friend

- **Intrapersonal Intelligence:** gifted at entrepreneurship, goal-setting, vision, and independence

- **Naturalist Intelligence:** gifted at nature, caring for pets, animals, tracking, or collecting

Armstrong argued that every child is a genius, not in the Einstein kind of way, but in the sense of the word's Greek and Latin origins. The word "genius" means "giving birth to one's joy." In other words, our children are geniuses at what brings them the most joy.

In education, then, "genius" essentially means "giving birth to the joy of learning." "Genius isn't awakened in a fancy kit or sophisticated syllabus," Armstrong wrote, "but in the simple but profound moments of an experience-rich childhood."[6]

Think about Frank Lloyd Wright, who fell in love with architecture by playing with blocks as a small child. Or Martha Graham, who found joy in dancing and choreography by watching a performance by Ruth St. Denis in Santa Barbara, California, when she was fourteen years old. Or Broadway star Ginna Claire Mason, who fell in love with acting when she saw *Wicked* as a child and later starred in the same show.[7]

Maybe you've heard about the painter Benjamin West, who, as a child, painted his little sister Sally's portrait using some bottles of ink. His mother walked by and said, "Why, it's Sally!" and kissed him. "My mother's kiss made me a painter," West said.[8]

"The gifts or qualities of genius that originate in childhood have the power to transform the world when they are carried into adulthood," Armstrong said.[9] This is why it's so important for parents to encourage and protect the genius of their children, even when it doesn't fit the conventional mold.

As parents, we stand as sentries at the gate of our children's hearts. We are the only ones who can spot their unique gifts and encourage them, because no one else knows our children like we do. It is up to us, as parents, to see the best in them, silence the naysayers, and protect the promising futures that await our kids.

This world doesn't need more of the same. Breakthroughs in every industry rely on fresh, innovative thinking that approaches problems from a different angle. The truth is, your unconventional, uniquely gifted children could very well be the revolutionaries we've been waiting for.

We don't need another Einstein. But we do need your children and the gift they will bring to their family, their community, and their world.

Covering a Multitude of Sins

"Our children do not need a makeover," the author Florence Littauer wrote. "They just need to be understood. If you understand their emotional needs now, you can save them a lifetime of searching for what they never had as a child."[10]

Understanding our kids can look like observing them as they grow, putting yourself in their shoes, and inviting them to share their perspectives. It can look like figuring out their personalities, decoding their learning styles, and uncovering their hidden strengths.

Understanding comes so often through smiles, little talks, and hugs. And sometimes it comes through mistakes, confusion, and hard conversations.

Understanding comes from asking difficult questions and sitting with our ability to be wrong. It requires reaching the end of ourselves and picking up where they begin. It is heartbreaks and heart bursts and everything in between. It is realizing, as they grow, that they don't merely change but become more themselves.

Understanding is deep and rich and altogether lovely.

Feeling understood can be more profound than love at times. After all, feeling understood tells us that we are loved and accepted and that we belong. It emboldens and empowers us to continue being and understanding ourselves. Studies show that being understood even protects us from depression.[11]

"Perhaps one did not want to be loved so much as to be understood," George Orwell wrote in *1984*.[12]

Love is unending, but our expressions can waver. Understanding brings us back to the basics. Back to our core values. Back to being a family committed for the long haul.

It is a privilege, a joy. It is our gift to each other.

In short, understanding our children is our great commission, for to be understood is to be loved.

You and I will keep making mistakes. We will fall back on bad habits. Heaven knows we will never be perfect. And yet we have been given this incredible responsibility of raising children anyway.

Let's commit to changing ourselves before trying to change our children.

Let's commit to healing from our childhoods before trying to perfect theirs.

Let's commit to understanding them and not simply diagnosing their struggles.

Our children don't merely want to be understood for how they express themselves through their personalities, temperaments, or talents. They want to be forgiven when they make mistakes. They want to be heard, known, and accepted. Most of all, our children want empathy.

Empathy covers a multitude of sins.

Notable author and professor Brené Brown said that "empathy has no script. There is no right or wrong way to do it. It's simply listening, holding space, withholding judgment, emotionally connecting, and communicating that incredibly healing message of 'you are not alone.'"[13]

We may not always understand our children. But showing them that we desire to understand is often enough to help them feel safe.

May we never let our child-rearing techniques get in the way of our children.

May we choose to be curious before we jump to conclusions.

May we seek to understand them in order to honor them.

And may we always remember that understanding is the greatest act of love.

5

TO CREATE
A SAFE HAVEN

If the family were a container,
it would be a nest, an enduring nest,
loosely woven, expansive, and open.

—LETTY COTTIN POGREBIN

My family has lived in a number of places we've called home. There was the urban townhouse where our boys learned to walk amid a maze of baby gates that blocked sets of stairs going every which way.

There was the cramped room with mattresses on the floor covered in plastic tarps to keep off the construction dust while a contractor refurbished the rest of the house.

The short-term rental that turned out to have an infestation of cockroaches and a landlord who refused to listen to reason. Oh, do I hate cockroaches. "Water bugs," she called them.

The custom-built condo we could no longer afford after the real estate market crashed.

The cookie-cutter, two-story house in north Georgia's suburbs that always smelled like curry.

And the family home we now enjoy, with a cozy book nook in our living room, an open floor plan for hosting friends, and a shaded refuge in the backyard for swimming, tree-climbing, and playing laser tag at night. Sure, it has too few bedrooms and not enough space for all the projects our imaginations dream up. And let's not talk about the lack of personal space. Still, it's home.

After all these experiences, I've come to realize something important: Homes are not built with our hands. They're made with our hearts.

My children have reminisced about memories made in some of the lowliest conditions.

Once, when my youngest boy was a baby, I scooped him out of his crib to find a dead cockroach in his hand. (Have I told you how much I hate cockroaches?) I still can't think about that experience without shuddering.

On top of that, it was the same year we experienced our greatest financial hardship, the testing of our marriage, and the terminal illness of my mother. I have an enormous sense of sadness from that entire season of life. I wish I could erase it from our history.

And yet, my children fondly recall their experiences in that place, the friends they made in the neighborhood, and our time together as a family—enjoying Saturday morning pancakes, splashing in puddles, and making our first family snow igloo during "Snowmageddon 2010."

It is proof that home is truly where the heart is.

Bruce Perry, a senior fellow of the Child Trauma Academy, said that it is far better to have a poverty of material things than a poverty of relationships.[1]

After many hardships, financial and otherwise, I'm so grateful this is true.

When hardship and misfortune strike, home is still there. When life throws its worst at you, home awaits. And when loneliness and isolation visit you for a season, home remains.

There have been times when my family was surrounded by friends, and other times when no one was around. There have been times when we couldn't pay the bills, and times when we could lavish our kids with surprises. No matter the circumstances, our life together has been a constant source of home.

We build our lives on the foundation of togetherness. We decorate the halls with laughter and furnish the rooms with sweet memories. We choose to travel the world with our children, rather than wait until they're grown and gone, and return to a place that feels like a harbor for our souls.

We watch the same movies together on Friday nights so we can repeat lines when they're home for the holidays in twenty years. And we treat each dinnertime as hallowed, so that the memory of meals and prayers and conversations together will sustain them until they have families of their own.

Home is a sanctuary. It's a sacred place where our children feel secure, learn about life, and unbridle their imaginations. We may not have control over a lot of things, but we can make our homes a safe haven for our kids. We can preserve childhood by protecting the environment in which it occurs.

The Greatest Gift We Can Give Our Children

The greatest gift we can give our children is to create a safe haven where they are free to be themselves apart from all the unnecessary input they would otherwise receive.

What is a safe haven? It's a place where they feel comfortable enough to explore who they are, to share their opinions, and to not be afraid of ridicule. A place where they can chase the harebrained ideas in their heads and experiment with a million different plans. A place where they can try on various versions of who they are and who they might want to become. A place where they can rest, hope, and dream.

A place where they can simply be.

I don't doubt my children's resilience or ability to walk confidently through life. But I know the toll that "too much, too soon" would take on them. The protective walls that would have to go up. The interests they would have to give up for the sake of "normalcy." The self-sabotage of their own creative expressions.

 I have enough faith in the peculiarities of my children to know they need to be protected from these things.

My thirteen-year-old taught himself to crochet last week, and now that the neighbors have new coasters and our friends have new placemats, he's working on a stuffed kitten for his sister.

It's amazing what a child will find fascinating when outside opinions are not a factor.

I wish I could say I taught him everything he knows, but that would be a far cry from the truth. The fact is that I fall short in many areas, even the ones that scream of my values. I'm learning, albeit slowly, to give myself grace, but I'm a work in progress, even there.

What I do know is that despite our shortcomings, kids still thrive. Perhaps they thrive *because* of our shortcomings.

With each passing day, I'm more grateful for the ways my shortcomings allow my children to shine. They may not all teach themselves to crochet. Some might need more from us to make it. Others might need more space to spread their wings. But all of them will learn to fly with ample amounts of curiosity, encouragement, and support.

The thing about childhood is that everything that matters to kids, especially in the teenage years—be it social ranking, athletic ability, physical appearance—means absolutely nothing in adulthood. If you don't believe me, check up on your high school classmates on Facebook. Time is the great equalizer. The once popular kids are pushing papers, spreading mulch, and growing bald spots, just like the rest of us.

Our job as parents is not to protect our children from all the pain, but to walk through it with them and provide age-appropriate protections along the way.

The trouble is that many parents assume it's their duty to help their kids "toughen up" by removing this safe haven. They push their children into difficult circumstances, thinking it will prepare them for "real life." They believe it's a rite of passage for their kids to be initiated like everybody else.

I used to volunteer in the church nursery when my eldest was a baby. There was a boy, about three years old, who cried from the instant his father dropped him off until he picked him up an hour later.

The other volunteers and I took turns holding him, trying to engage him in play, but mostly consoling him and helping him feel secure. After several weeks, the father gave us new instructions. "Please don't hold him today if he cries," he said firmly. "He needs to learn how to make it through. He needs to toughen up."

My heart sank. I knew this boy and his family. I knew he needed a little extra love during a rough season for his parents. There was nothing that could have kept me from consoling that child.

Parents mean well. But in an effort to "toughen up" their children, they only make them feel more insecure. When we take away their safe haven, our kids have to fight for survival both when they're out in the world and also at home.

Never mind that life is tough enough on its own. That there are plenty of opportunities for our children to develop a thick skin without feeling utterly abandoned by their parents. That being ridiculed or pushed around doesn't actually strengthen a person but can cause serious harm.

In her book *For the Family's Sake*, author Susan Schaeffer Macaulay wrote:

> For many of us, the word home brings warm thoughts and happy memories—far more than the dictionary's simple definition of "a place of birth or one's living quarters." For many of us, home is where the heart is. Yet it is even more than that. It is the secure environment that allows our hearts to develop. A haven of growth, quiet, and rest. The place where we love and are loved.
>
> Sadly though, this kind of home is beginning to disappear as our busy society turns homes into houses where related people abide, but there is no "heart."[2]

Our task isn't to prepare children for the challenges of life by making their home life difficult. It's to give them a safe, nurturing space to be their true selves, for only then can they truly thrive.

After all, as T. S. Eliot said, "home is where one starts from."[3]

Heartsteading

You may have heard of homesteaders, but my friend Stephanie Beaty is a "heartsteader." She turns every home into a safe haven for her children. It might have something to do with her husband Mike's military career, which forced them to live in fourteen different homes in eighteen years. But Stephanie has poured herself into creating warm, inviting spaces where her children can feel safe and have a sense of belonging.

When she lived in Richmond, Virginia, I often drove the two hours to her house, where there was a climbing wall installed in her living room, monkey bars going up the underside of her spiral staircase, a wicker chair that hung from the rafters, and a set of vintage school lockers in the kitchen where her children could store their belongings. These weren't all professional installations, but rather items she found on Facebook and in salvage stores.

What's more, Stephanie gives her children the space to just be kids. Whether it's a shared bunk room with a view of the river from their tiny river cottage in Florida or the zip line through the trees at their house in the big woods in Virginia, her children will always know that their childhood was cherished.

Beginning in the summer of 2018, the Beaty family took it one step further by spending an unforgettable year and a half on the road. They traded in their forty-five-hundred-square-foot home for a thirty-two-foot Class C motorhome to begin a sabbatical they affectionately referred to as "the family field trip." After serving two decades as a navy family and spending more time apart than together, they yearned for unhurried, intentional time as a family.

They had saved up for a family gap year after Mike's military retirement and decided to spend the next eighteen months traveling twelve thousand miles, seeing some of the most majestic parts of the country, and growing closer together than they ever imagined possible.

"Of course, there were hurdles, mechanical (and emotional) breakdowns, and a few more sewer issues than we'd like to recount," Stephanie said. "But we learned that life isn't as much what happens to you as how you respond to it."

Stephanie and her family finally returned to their hometown in Florida, where they purchased a small, river cottage and are settling in for the next season of life together. Their eighteen-month road trip brought them closer together and made up for lost time after a season of being apart.

"A season of travel, rest, and adventures helped us give attention to the people and practices that mattered most to us," Stephanie said.

Your life circumstances may not allow for a year-long road trip, but maybe you have a month, a weekend, or even an afternoon to pour into your family.

"You can take a vacation or a staycation," Stephanie said. "You can camp in a national park or your own backyard. Work with what is available to you. You may be surprised that it is more than enough."

You don't need a big house or an expensive one to create a safe haven.

You need only a little creativity and a penchant for contentment.

Create a Comfortable Space

"Hygge" (pronounced "hue-guh") is a Danish word used to describe a moment or feeling of coziness and comfort. There isn't one English word that accurately describes hygge, but many would say it is more of a mood than a moment, more of a feeling than a fad. You don't define it as much as you feel it.

Similarly, raising your kids the wild and free way will always be hard to describe. Intentional living will always be more than something you do. It's an atmosphere you create, a lifestyle you cultivate with small intentional acts of comfort, delight, and joy. In short, you don't define it, you feel it.

The goal of delightful learning isn't simply to get cozy with candles, cardigans, and cocoa (although that would be reason enough for me). The goal is to create a feeling of contentment and well-being in order to promote optimal heart and mind stimulation. Brain research has long shown that stress impairs learning. Plain and simple, if children are stressed, they will not learn.

Hygge might sound a bit like fluff, a fad that found its way into our home-making culture for a season. But no matter what you call it, hygge is essential to living and learning at home.

When we go the extra mile to create a safe haven for our children, we aren't coddling them. We are encouraging their minds to learn, grow, and eventually soar. Studies show that a child's comfort level is directly related to their ability to transmit and store information in the brain.

The secret lies not in the warm drinks, comforting stories, and cozy blankets, but in the delight and passion that these practices evoke, the community it conjures within our homes.

My friend Sara Beth knows the key to keeping her teens around more often is to make their home a warm and welcoming place for their friends to hang out. They move frequently, so the first thing she does in each new home is to hang twinkle lights around an outdoor table and turn the nearest room into a cozy lounge area for rainy days and Sunday afternoon sports-watching. She volunteers to host everything from pre-event parties to post-event photo shoots. It doesn't take long for her home to be known as the fun house, and her photos always include a gaggle of teens, most of whom are not her own.

If you want to create an environment that welcomes kids, meet them where they are. Foster a place where your children's friends love to gather. Celebrate the same traditions every week, like pizza on Friday nights and bike rides on Saturday mornings. Put a time limit on technology. Create a place for dirty hiking boots by the back door to encourage a lifestyle of exploring nature. And arrange your living room based on how you want it to be used, not how it looks on Instagram.

But above all else, furnish your house with love. Cultivate a spirit of joy each morning with homemade pancakes and music. Read stories by J. R. R. Tolkien and C. S. Lewis before bedtime to fill your children's heads with adventure as they fall asleep. Put chickens in the backyard to foster kindness and caretaking, or perhaps just comic relief. Make acceptance your creed; and smiles, your secret sauce.

If anything can be said of our homes, may it be that they are safe places for our children. Places where they can be encouraged in their gifts and comforted in their struggles. Places where they can share their fears and express their sorrows. Places where they can be heard and known and taken seriously. We create a safe haven for our family because children thrive when they feel safe, but also because this is love.

Love Is the Safe Haven They Need

Family is where our children derive their identity. It's where they learn inside jokes, the cheat codes to board games from Dad, and their favorite meals from Mama. Or vice versa.

It's where they learn how to drive and swear at the car that just cut them off. (Sorry, kids.) It's where they grow up listening to music that becomes the soundtrack of their childhoods.

Families are the source of that pesky inner voice that tells them what they can and cannot do. They're the source of countless memories that guide them as they raise children of their own.

But families can also be the source of the greatest pain a child will ever know. Sometimes it's blatant, like physical or sexual abuse, abandonment, emotional trauma, and name-calling. Other times it's the unspoken words that strike deep into a child's heart and never surface until they have a family of their own, limping and broken, trying to become a better version of their parents, to no avail.

All of us have wounds from our childhoods. Wounds we didn't know we could be angry about because we were still trying to figure out what was normal and what was wrong. Wounds that resurface at the most inopportune times in our lives—like when we're raising precious, little souls of our own.

But a great reckoning has come to the parents of our generation. Fathers no longer stand outside the room while their wives deliver babies inside. We're privy to the consequences of our pain. We have been confronted with the sobering reality that these wounds have been passed down from generation to generation, and it's up to us to figure out what to do with them.

Our greatest challenge is to not let our wounds affect our kids and to break these cycles once and for all.

Society tries to medicate the hurts right out of us. But that only numbs us, makes us functioning parents at best. It doesn't heal us. Society also gives us distractions that help us ignore the pain. Substances. A career to pursue. A busy schedule to keep. A good divorce lawyer. The "block" button on Instagram.

We manage the hurts for as long as we can, convincing each other that we're being good parents by abiding together. We console ourselves with the notion that at least we love our children and our children love us, no matter how they act or what kind of day we've had.

But before long, the pressures of life catch up with our households. We find ourselves confronted with an enemy that lies not only without, but also within, and also around us.

Yes, there are times when our children can cause us great pain. They stoke the anger and fuel the discouragement we already fight so hard to suppress. We have the power to discipline our kids for behaviors that inflame the wounds already within us.

It is in these moments that society's solutions will destroy us. They will destroy our households and our families too. But the solutions society offers are far easier to choose because the cure is so much harder to embrace.

The cure has always been, and always will be, love.

"Love is patient, love is kind," an ancient rabbi once wrote. "It does not envy, it does not boast, it is not proud. It does not dishonor others, it is not self-seeking, it is not easily angered, it keeps no record of wrongs."[4]

How do we love and thus create a safe haven for our children?

First, we address our own need for healing—from childhood trauma, emotional neglect, external stressors like poverty, adoption, or systemic racism, just to name a few.

This is the hard part—facing our past hurts and confronting our present mistakes because of them—because it requires us to relive them.

Second, we lay down our weapons—our words, our training techniques, our quick fixes—and pick up the mantle of love and empathy and the capacity to hold space for our children. We hold space for their undesirable behavior, their insecurities, and their outbursts because they're dealing with their own hurts and wounds and are struggling to know how to process them.

And third, we provide them with a home that's like a nest—enduring, loosely woven, expansive, and open—that can hold them in love while they are becoming who they were meant to be.

But to raise whole children, we must become whole versions of ourselves. "Whole," in this sense, doesn't mean perfect. That would be impossible. And it doesn't mean we aren't lacking in certain areas or don't still need to grow in many more.

"Whole" means that when we see ourselves in our children's behavior, we look to heal that part of ourselves rather than lash out in anger.

Being whole means being able to acknowledge that our children's misalignment isn't an assault on us, but rather a result of their own becoming, then responding in acceptance and love.

Creating a safe haven starts with us.

Love, as it turns out, is the safest place of all.

Further Reading

Sometimes, restoring a sense of safety for our children calls for more than our own reserves allow. To save our kids' childhoods, we must first heal our own. If you don't feel safe with yourself or others, please know you are not alone. For help, reach out to a trauma-informed therapist. There are also many wonderful resources that exist if you'd like to explore this journey further. Here are a few:

- *The Body Keeps the Score: Brain, Mind, and Body in the Healing of Trauma* by Bessel van der Kolk, MD

- *No Bad Parts: Healing Trauma and Restoring Wholeness with the Internal Family Systems Model* by Richard C. Schwartz, PhD

- *The Return to Ourselves: Trauma, Healing, and the Myth of Normal* by Dr. Gabor Maté

- *Waking the Tiger: Healing Trauma* by Peter A. Levine, PhD

- *What Happened to You? Conversations on Trauma, Resilience, and Healing* by Bruce D. Perry, MD, PhD, and Oprah Winfrey

6

TO REDEEM WHAT'S BEEN BROKEN

*We do not have to be qualified
to be whole or healed.*

—MADELEINE L'ENGLE

There is a perception about Wild + Free that, in trying to preserve childhood for our own kids, we are trying to replicate the euphoria of the childhoods we experienced ourselves. As if, by reading *Anne of Green Gables* or the Little House on the Prairie books, we are trying to relive our personal experiences.

But nothing could be further from the truth.

Some of the most loving and inspiring mamas I know grew up in the homes of abusive alcoholics, experienced rape, suffered through addictions, harmed themselves, or endured trauma as young children. Many of them carry dark and shameful secrets they wish to hide from everyone, especially their own kids, to say nothing of their own struggling marriages, broken family bonds, and untamed tendencies.

No, our desire to preserve childhood for the next generation is not born out of some idyllic fancy, but rather a personal mission to restore what has been lost in our own lives.

In truth, many of us have at least a few things we long to re-create from our own childhoods. Whether it's family dinners, favorite vacation spots, or beloved traditions, there are simple moments that have been etched into the grooves of our brains, making us who we are today.

Some of us want to give our children all the good things we had growing up. Others want to give our children all the things we didn't have. Perhaps there's a little of both in all of us.

What is most important, however, is that we give our children what they need. And for most of us, this requires redeeming some of the brokenness of our past.

This is the beautiful calling of parenthood: to do for our children what they cannot do for themselves.

Our hearts may not be entirely pieced together. We may have scars and wounds that run deep in our souls, but we can at least give our children parents who are healing, redeeming what's been broken, and becoming whole.

What a noble endeavor. What a worthy calling. Childhood memories are a mixed bag of magical moments and heavy heartaches. Who can forget running through freshly cut grass each summer to dive onto a Slip 'N Slide? Who can forget the sights and sounds of backyard barbecues with checkered tablecloths, watermelon slices as big as your face, and the aroma of hamburgers and hot dogs on the grill? Who can forget scooping ice cream cones on grandpa and grandma's porch after an exhilarating game of tag with all the cousins?

Childhood possesses the best of everything this life has to offer.

But for many kids, childhood ends too soon. They're forced to hide in closets while a screaming match takes place downstairs. They're forced to grow up too fast when one parent abandons the family or the younger children are neglected and left alone. Mental illness, addiction, or disability strike the household, and suddenly the children are required to fill their parents' shoes long before it's time.

I remember when my parents first got divorced and my younger brother and I were shuttled back and forth between two states to satisfy the visitation rights. I held my trembling little brother in my arms to help him fall asleep at night and coaxed him to breathe through the overwhelming anxiety.

The question for all of us is this: At what moment were we forced to graduate from childlike innocence into the harsh realities of this broken world? At what point did we realize that our circumstances didn't look like anyone else's? When did we realize that our fathers didn't act like other dads? (Or our mothers, for that matter?) When did we discover that not all family friends, uncles, or cousins were safe? When did we give up on the wonder and innocence of childhood, harden our hearts, and resolve to never go back?

My guess is that, whenever it occurred, it was far too soon.

We all have hopes for this parenting journey we're on. We're passionate about doing some things a certain way and not doing other things at all. But our upbringing has *everything* to do with how we parent. Pam Leo calls this our "parenting inheritance."[1]

Our parents did the best they could with what they knew and what they had. We can see the sacrifices they made and the meaningful experiences they gave us and know that it took real intention on their part to break from the past. They made a way of escape for us out of their own harmed histories, and for that, we are grateful. We can reclaim those good things for our own children.

But there are also things we wish had been different. Things we're struggling to overcome. Experiences we wish we would've had. Connections we craved. Opportunities they couldn't afford. Decisions we didn't agree with. Disciplinary tactics that hurt us. The list goes on.

All parenting is a mixture of the instinctual and the intentional. The instinctual is wonderful when we come from good homes, but it can be devastating when we're fighting the tragedies of our upbringing. When this happens, it takes real effort to break the cycle and begin a new way with our children.

This is our holy mandate: to redeem the bad and reclaim the good.

Ending Harmful Cycles

I have a dear friend who struggled with anger and sought counseling to find a cure. She went to a therapist and asked, "How do I stop blowing up at my kids and my spouse?"

The anger, she believed, stemmed from a painful childhood: both of her parents were too aloof to meet a deep craving for love inside her. She had learned to argue and lash out as a way to get attention from them, and she was repeating the same harmful cycle with her own family.

The counselor told her to regulate her breathing and to identify the warning signs of anger before they manifested. She left his office and never went back because his solution was too simple for her complicated issue. She needed more than a coping mechanism. She needed a cure and determined to find someone who would give her problem the attention it required.

The second counselor she visited asked a few probing questions and listened for a while before she leaned forward and gave a direct answer. It was neither shock therapy nor prescription medication.

"You can end this," the counselor said. "You simply have to decide that you will not do it any longer. And then together we can work on the underlying reasons behind it."

It reminded me of the old Bob Newhart spoof of a psychiatrist who yells at his patient, "Stop it!" If you haven't seen the skit, it's ancient but worth an internet search.

My friend nearly walked away from this counselor too but decided to give it a try. By being intentional about not lashing out in anger, she was able to overcome the urge and then begin to work on healing the underlying cause behind it.

The work of healing takes time, and not every solution is this simple. But some things aren't as complicated as we make them out to be.

Taking responsibility for our actions and changing our behaviors can start with one decision. What can you vow to stop today?

I vow to stop comparing my children to other kids in conversation with them.

I vow to stop worrying that my kids are "behind" and focus on where they are and what they need.

I vow to stop asking my children to do things they can't do.

I vow to stop judging myself and offer grace for my mistakes and imperfections.

If our instinctual parenting cannot be trusted because of established patterns, then we have to be intentional about reacting differently. We have to act in ways that defy our emotions.

What if we didn't have to react to every emotion, every outburst, or every disrespectful comment? What if we held space for big emotions without taking offense? What if we chose not to "parent" every little thing out of them? What if we trusted the process of "living and loving big" together a little bit more?

It's more than just picking our battles. It's deciding that the culprit is not our children, but the cause of their behavior. And it's choosing love as our tool to respond to it.

When we decide to address every negative behavior in our children or, more destructively, express every negative emotion that we feel about their behavior, we are choosing to rule them rather than have a relationship with them.

Laura Markham, the author of *Peaceful Parent, Happy Kids*, wrote, "Every negative interaction with your child uses up valuable relationship capital."[2]

I fail at modeling this almost every single day in some way or another. But I truly believe that kindness is the cure. And not reacting in an outburst is the new, bold love. It takes restraint. It takes patience. It takes intention to weigh the cost before tipping the scales.

You are not your mistakes. Your children are not their shortcomings. Ditch the lies that leave you stuck in fateful thinking and that keep you from seeing the promise of this beautiful life.

Lies destroy. Love restores.

Lies see failure. Love seizes possibilities.

Lies hold you back. Love sets you free.

Healing from the Past

Some wounds run so deep that they alter the psyche and leave trauma in the mind, heart, and body. We don't always want to admit these hurts because acknowledging them conjures up such immense grief, pain, and maybe even anger. It feels better to keep them buried inside, to leave those stones unturned.

We're only human, we tell ourselves. *Nobody's perfect.*

The trouble is that we continue to parent our children from instinct—what we know and have always known—which isn't necessarily healthy or helpful. And we do nothing to stop the cycle of dysfunction from recurring again and again through our children and our children's children.

Did you know that we, as mothers, carry our grandchildren in our own wombs?

It's true. As women, we are formed in the womb with all the eggs we will ever possess. This means that if we give birth to daughters, we also carry the eggs of our future grandchildren. So our lives began inside of our grandmothers, and our grandchildren begin their lives inside of us.

It's a beautifully scandalous thought to know we are a part of our ancestors and they are a part of us in this way. But this means we can also carry the same dysfunctions and tendencies of our grandparents and influence the kinds of conditions that our grandchildren and great-grandchildren will inherit.

Even if you were adopted or haven't given birth, science now supports the fact that our experiences become a part of our biology.[3] Everything from physical disease to emotional trauma can be passed on through our DNA.[4]

Maybe you've let the horror of your history impact the environment of your home. You can still change the future for your children.

It all starts with you. Right now. Today.

Dr. Gabor Maté said, "Trauma is not what happened to you. It is what happens inside you."[5] This means we can heal. If trauma is a wound, then we can heal it. We can heal it for us. And we can heal it for our children.

I highly recommend meeting with a professional counselor, particularly a trauma-informed therapist, to work through the pain of your past. I've done it for years, and it's been crucial to helping me overcome certain challenges. I am not a therapist. I am not trained to counsel you, and I won't assume that I know what you need.

What I do know from my personal journey and research is that healing from past hurts is critical to creating the kind of family culture we desire and passing on a beautiful hope for future generations. As Dr. Will Cole wrote, "If trauma can be passed on through generations, then so can healing."[6]

The first step is acknowledging your wounds. When you identify them, you're able to understand where your toxic behaviors are coming from. I have to warn you, though, that by revisiting the past, you'll likely be overcome with feelings of grief, anger, and betrayal over what was taken from you.

These feelings only get worse as you replace toxic reactions with healthy ones. By refusing to respond with an instinctive crutch like anger, apathy, or distraction, you'll feel the pain even more.

By nature, we try to avoid heavy emotions at all costs, which is why we bury them with alternative, unhealthy expressions in the first place. Workaholism. Alcoholism. Violent tempers. Rage and anger. Physical and emotional abuse. Neglect. The list goes on.

But feeling the depths of this despair is the beginning of your healing journey. You have to work through the emotions in all the proper ways and deal with each one as it comes along. It won't be easy. It may be the hardest thing you've ever done. You may want to give up and go back to the way things were before. But don't do it. Take the steps that will alter the course of your family for generations to come.

Healing from the past is not only important for our own souls. Our children's futures are at stake.

You may not be able to eradicate every hurt and dysfunction that came from your childhood. You're still going to slip up, regress, make mistakes, and do things you swore you'd never repeat. But you can heal from the past and lessen the blow.

Pam Leo wrote, "Every generation of parents softens what they got for their children. If what we got was harsh, imagine what our parents got. We parent our children best when we can forgive, heal, and not pass on hurts."[7]

If hurt people hurt people, then healed people can heal people.

What have you been unwilling to confront in the name of being imperfectly human? What would you be willing to face from your past for the sake of your children's futures? What would it look like to heal from your past wounds, your ancestors' wrongdoings, or your current injustices? What would it look like to heal together?

Restoring Relationships

On the other side of childhood, an uncertain future awaits. There is so much complexity in our world for children to unravel. We raise them the best we can but pass along our own mistakes, handed down from imperfect parents. We intend to act as a dam, holding back the force of our pasts, only allowing the best to come through, giving life and power to our own homes. But sometimes the force is too strong. Sometimes the dam breaks.

Other times, the fault lies not with us but in circumstances over which we have no control. A friend of our family recounted the time when a sexual molester was caught giving candy to young boys in exchange for taking certain liberties at the church where he volunteered. Our friend remembered seeing his own son with a lollipop after the service several weeks prior without any explanation of where he got it, and terror filled his mind at the thought of what might have happened.

We release our children into the world on a wing and a prayer with the underlying belief that most people are good. And indeed, they are. But I also know that my childhood was filled with experiences, exposures, and close calls to which my parents were not privy, and still aren't to this day.

Sometimes the brokenness of childhood is manifested in severed family relationships. I know more and more adults who have cut their parents out of their lives to avoid dysfunction. Their children don't know their grandparents, and they go through every major holiday without them.

Sometimes young adults leave home and never look back, making a different way of life for themselves and their new families. The kids are the real losers in all this, as they become detached from their family history and lose their sense of belonging, not to mention additional love and support.

The result of brokenness is more brokenness.

Will the circle ever be unbroken?

It doesn't have to be this way. I believe this wild and free generation is the one that can turn the tide of their families for generations to come. I believe you and I can do something about it.

Healing comes after we acknowledge our hurts. And after healing comes restoration. This is the hard part—restoring relationships—because no one wants to forgive their oppressor. No one wants to forgive the one who has hurt or hindered a child, especially when that child was us.

But forgiveness is the only way to fully heal from our past trauma, bridge the chasm in our hearts, and put our lives back together. To do otherwise is to perpetuate pain through generations to come.

A Family Reunion

On Thanksgiving Day, my family zipped along the backroads of rural Ohio surrounded by farms and cornfields as far as the eye could see. We had traveled fourteen hours to get here, our nervous Pomeranian in tow, our trunk filled with ready-to-bake turkey, mashed potatoes, gravy, and pumpkin pies from Cracker Barrel. It would have been like any other holiday with family, except our family didn't know we were coming. We had never spent Thanksgiving with them before.

Whatever wounds happened in my husband Ben's heart as a child, this was the year he decided to restore some relationships. We parked along the street to his parents' house so he could call them ahead of our ambush and make sure they were home. They were. They were watching Hallmark Christmas movies.

We crept along the street as he exchanged pleasantries and pulled into the driveway. "What are we doing? Oh, just running an errand," Ben said.

"To where?" they asked.

"An undisclosed location."

"An undisclosed location?"

We snuck out of the car and rang the doorbell.

"Hold on a minute," they said. "Someone's at the door."

The seven of us and Clementine the Pomeranian piled together like carolers on the front stoop, our arms filled with the Thanksgiving bounty. Ben's father looked through the window.

"You're never going to believe who it is," he said, opening the door.

We yelled, "Surprise!" And as we embraced, tears fell.

My two girls, eight and five, ran ahead of the pack to give their grandparents a big embrace—the grandparents they had never met before.

Reclaiming the Good

There is always good to be reclaimed from our pasts, even in the hardest of circumstances. The problem is that we can't always separate the bad from the good . . . until we heal, that is. Healing is a miraculous state of being that occurs when you recall a painful memory but, knowing that you are on a healing journey, don't dwell on it. You acknowledge it, deal with it, forgive it if necessary, and then move on.

Moving on is possible when you decide that dwelling on the hurt doesn't help your healing.

Reclaiming the good from our past is important to creating the future we desire. The memories of your childhood, of splashing in creeks and chasing fireflies in the fields. The memories of your mother making pancakes on Saturday morning or your father building a playset in the backyard. The stories of your parents' childhoods, the story of how they met, and the story of your birth. The stories of your grandparents who immigrated to America to give their family a better life.

Pain and tragedy may be interwoven through their stories, but it is the good we choose to reclaim from the past that makes our stories worth telling, the stories of your history but also your legacy.

When the pain of the past still holds us in bondage, we can't tell these stories freely. We can't remember them without remembering the bad. But when we begin to heal, to let our hearts heal, to decide which memories are worth holding on to, we can begin to reclaim the good.

Our parents' histories do not need to define our own stories, let alone those of our grandparents or great-grandparents. They might have played a part in how we came to be, but any wound that still exists can heal if we let it. We can reclaim a different path for our families.

We cannot undo what has been done in the past. But perhaps we can learn from it, understand it, and change to reflect the kind of future we want to create.

Perhaps that is what makes life beautiful.

Rewriting the Future

Alice Walker, the author of *The Color Purple*, wrote, "Look closely at the present you are constructing: it should look like the future you are dreaming."[8]

So, friends, what does the future you are dreaming look like?

If you want your children to be happy, show them happiness now.

If you want your children to speak up for themselves, let them have a voice now.

If you want your children to be peacemakers, show them how to restore conflict now.

If you want your children to come home one day, let your heart be a home to them now.

If you want your children to move mountains, let them move and shake and challenge now.

If you want your children to be free from generational cycles, do the work to break them now.

We may not have the power to change the past, but we possess a much greater one: the ability to create a different future for our children. It starts with breaking generational patterns.

Maybe it's neglect. Maybe it's a raging temper. Maybe it's a controlling nature. Maybe it's physical abuse. Maybe it's not saying "I love you." Maybe it's shaming. Maybe it's comparison to others. Maybe it's setting unattainable expectations. Maybe it's making others work for love. Maybe it's codependency.

Sometimes generational patterns don't manifest as they were received. For example, children who are shamed for their emotions grow up to become adults with a backlog of pain that still needs to come out. Children whose core needs for attachment as infants are neglected grow up to become adults who don't know how to attach or relate in healthy ways. Children who live in volatile homes grow up to become adults who can only function through dysfunction and discord.

Identifying toxic generational patterns doesn't mean that we will suddenly stop doing them. It takes time. It takes work. But it is the most important work, and it is time well spent.

Wouldn't you rather give the gift of freedom to your children than make them work for it themselves?

Author and children's rights advocate L. R. Knost wrote:

We have to break the cycle of hurting children to raise children. Hurting children grow up to believe that children deserve to be hurt, that they MUST be hurt to be raised well. And thus generational pain is passed along. But, sometimes, hurting children grow up and recognize the destructive pattern. They do the work to heal themselves and to find ways to raise their children peacefully. And the generational pain cycle is broken. This is our time, our chance to heal ourselves and to heal the future. Let's choose the path of peace, my friends. Let's break the cycle, not the child. Let's change the world, one little heart at a time.[9]

Our children will have their own work to do as they become adults and make their own mistakes. And there will certainly be things we didn't get right that they will have to redeem and reclaim, as well.

But let's do our part while we still can. Don't leave your children to pick up the pieces on their own. Don't sacrifice your discomfort on the altar of their future marriage and family.

Let's do the work now.

Let's do it together.

Let's ask ourselves questions like "Does this behavior support the environment I'm trying to create? Does this behavior support the childhood I want them to have? Does this behavior support the life we're trying to create together?"

Let's build a future for our children that's so strong that they can be courageous in their brave new world.

Our culture today is filled with casualties left on the battlefield of an invisible war—a war within families, a war within hearts and homes. But I have a feeling that the world our children help create will need more than shell-shocked casualties. It will need revolutionaries. And it starts with us. It starts with awareness, followed by deliberate actions that move us forward, one step at a time.

This is messy business, but there's no time for guilt or shame, regret or remorse. It's not going to be pretty, but the payoff will be priceless. At times it may feel like a cacophony. But if you listen closely, you'll hear a symphony—the soundtrack to a story of the broken becoming whole.

When we do the work of breaking generational patterns, the reward is the freedom we receive on the other side of it. There are no good parents and bad parents, only broken people doing the best they can. But we don't have to live in the brokenness of the past.

Our great hope is not in the here and now, but it is here and now that we stop the cycles keeping our families in bondage. It is here and now that our children's stories are rewritten in the stars, their future families handed a new hope.

No matter your brokenness, no matter your mistakes, there is nothing keeping you from becoming whole, of redeeming the brokenness of your past or even your family's past.

You don't have to be perfect to take the first steps.

You don't have to be qualified to be whole or healed.

All it takes is you, whole and healed, redeeming the good.

7

TO CHASE
WONDER

*All of us have wonders hidden
in our breasts, only needing
circumstances to evoke them.*

—CHARLES DICKENS

I n 1965, an image of a young woman sitting in the tall grasses in Gombe, in Africa, among a community of chimpanzees appeared on the cover of *National Geographic* magazine.

Without any formal academic training, the twenty-six-year-old set foot in the forests of what is now Tanzania to observe chimpanzees in the wild. She immersed herself in their habitat and came to know them as unique individuals with distinct personalities and complex emotions.

Her discovery that chimps make and use tools is considered one of the greatest scholarly achievements of the twentieth century.

Now, nearly ninety years old, Jane Goodall is still hard at work as a conservationist and activist in Africa, speaking all over the world in hope of building a better future for our children.

Jane grew up loving animals and dreaming of going to Africa to live among them. But she wasn't a world traveler—she was just a girl from Bournemouth, England, who had a deep bond with the beech tree in her backyard. She would climb up into its branches to daydream, heaving books up in a basket with a rope so she could read.

She called the tree "one of my closest childhood friends."[1]

Jane described a naturalist as someone who "looks for the wonder of nature. Listens to the voice of nature and learns from nature, trying to understand it." She said, "As a naturalist, you need to have empathy, intuition, and love. You need to be prepared to look at a murmuration of starlings and be filled with awe at the amazing agility of these birds. How do they fly in a flock of thousands and not touch at all and yet have such close formations and swoop and fly together, almost as one? And why do they do it? For fun? For joy?"[2]

Jane didn't discover her calling with extravagant trips around the world or university classes, but by quietly chasing wonder high from the branches of a beech tree, which she affectionately called Beech, in the quiet garden of her childhood.

Jane said this of her experience: "A sense of calm came over me. More and more often I found myself thinking, this is where I belong. This is what I came into this world to do."[3]

Our children don't need much, just the opportunity to create futures forged in the trenches of wonder-steeped childhoods.

We don't just chase wonder as an ulterior motive for learning.
We don't just chase wonder as another task on our to-do list.

We don't just chase wonder because wonder leads to wisdom (although it does).

We don't just chase wonder for Instagram likes or bragging rights.

We chase wonder because it's the thing we want to do most in the world.

We chase wonder because it is how we know our place in the world.

We chase wonder because it is the way we belong to the world.

We chase wonder because wonder-chasers change the world.

How Wonder Works

We have been conditioned to believe that if we don't force children to learn, they won't do it. But that is the exact opposite of how learning works. Wonder is the spark of learning. And a child's desire to learn cannot be fanned into flame without it. Our job is to protect that spark, preserve it, and keep it alive and well.

My friend and Wild + Free mama Katrien Van Deuren said, "Learning isn't just about being served the right amount of information. It's about diving into stories and becoming part of them. It is the joy of discovering how things work and of adventuring through mechanisms and truths and making them your own. Through learning, we bridge the gap between ourselves and the world that surrounds us."[4]

Even science supports a wonder-filled approach to learning.

We know that spending time in nature improves our cognitive abilities and benefits children with ADHD and spectrum disorders.[5] We know that play is the primary engine of growth in human beings.[6] We know that when children move, it helps them learn.[7] We know that children need to learn with all their senses and not just words and text.[8] And we know that the instant we tell children something, we take away the opportunity for them to learn it themselves.[9]

Nothing is learned, Jean Piaget said, unless the child discovers it for himself.[10] When we focus on fostering wonder, we have to put down our metrics and lay aside our desire to test, track, and label. We have to trust the process over the product. Our kids will find their way.

Show me a child who's been taught to think for himself, and I'll show you a world changer.

Show me a child who's been allowed to bloom at her own pace, and I'll show you a grounded and confident leader.

Show me a child raised in nature, and I'll show you a happier and more creative thinker.

Show me a child who's been given copious amounts of time to play and get lost in his imagination, and I'll show you an innovator with greater emotional intelligence.

Let's restore what's been lost in our children's education. Wonder. Story. Play. Curiosity. Nature. The essence of a living education. Let's give our kids a lifetime of learning at their fingertips and create a thinking, reading, and soul-filling culture in our homes.

Stop worrying about whether you have what it takes to teach your children all the things. You don't have to be an expert. You only need to prepare the path for exploration.

Robert Frost said, "I am not a teacher, but an awakener."[11] Let's be awakeners of wonder.

Wonder Schooling

Wonder lives in every child. It drives them to open their eyes each morning like it's the first time they've seen the world. It causes them to try new things and sparks their curiosity to explore the world around them. It makes them run down hills shrieking in delight or flee from crashing waves in gleeful terror.

Wonder encourages them to jump in rain puddles and chase fireflies at dusk. It provokes them to tears at the discovery of a lifeless bird and compels them to watch a spider build its web with equal fascination and fright. Wonder is found in gardens, clouds, and fields of buttercups. Wonder is the life force of learning. It's every child's birthright. The catalyst for curiosity. And the impetus for discovery.

I must warn you, though. Wonder is not neat and tidy or perfectly packaged for the partaking. It's often messy, unorganized, and intangible.

It requires us to prioritize exploration over efficiency.

It asks us to respect discovery over "done."

And it invites us to trust the process over the end product.

Let's hold on to that "holy curiosity," as Einstein called it.[12]

As parents, we have to be curious too. We are the ones who must awaken wonder in our children. We are the ones who must research and uncover the tools to teach and raise whole children.

We are the ones who must give our children fewer absolutes and more freedom to explore. We are the ones to let them be little. The ones to let them ask why. The ones to take them to the meadows and marvel at the wildflowers. The ones to show them the moon each night and point out the stars.

We are the ones who must open good books with them and read until our throats are dry and aching. The ones to stop what we're doing and engage them in conversation. The ones to lie in the grass on our backs and spot shapes in the clouds. The ones to look up from our screens and deep into their wide eyes. We are the ones to see that the world is one giant wonder, once again.

Beware the doubt that looms over every parent's head. Ignore the nagging feeling that you're not doing enough. The success of what we do lies in our love for our children and our commitment to seeing them grow into who they were made to be.

A final destination isn't our goal but rather a future worth living for our children. And this can only be found in the faithfulness of doing our best. The deep work of the soul happens beneath the surface, where the dew of wonder cannot be scorched by blazes of morning sunlight and the buds of ideas cannot be trampled before they are fully formed.

The daily rhythms that offer peace in an uncertain world . . . the familiar spaces that offer a haven to growing hearts . . . the deep dives that offer the chance to develop passions . . . the lessons learned in the slow, sun-soaked days of childhood . . . the imaginations formed and the relationships forged in the magical mundane—though the struggles are many, the blessings are countless on this wild and free journey.

No, you won't get it all right. We're all human. We learn and grow, just the same as our kids. But you can do this. You were made for this.

Chasing Wonder Together

I know what you're thinking. We're parents. Mothers and fathers. Unpaid instructors and unappreciated teachers. We are boo-boo kissers and sticky-face holders. We are short-order cooks and stinky-towel launderers. We are potty-trainers and homework checkers and bed-time managers. We are heart-wrung worriers and do-anything-for-them lovers.

We are tired and overwhelmed and carrying our own bag of burdens. And now we have to add chasing wonder to our list of duties? Sigh.

No wonder no one chases wonder. There's just no time.

But I beg you, implore you, to make time for wonder.

Kids don't need another box to check, a circle to fill in, or a Zoom video to watch. They don't need more information stuffed into their heads or another test to take to track their progress. Kids need someone to believe in them, love them, and walk alongside them to uncover wisdom, truth, and beauty.

They need time to play, time to think, and time to grow at their own pace. They need to fall in love with learning once again and believe that the world has more to offer than an assembly line of lessons to fulfill them. They need what poet and educator E. Merrill Root described as "a renaissance of wonder."[13]

They need us—their parents, teachers, and caregivers—to reclaim the wonder in education. The wonder of living and learning. The wonder of childhood.

Here are some ways you can chase wonder with your children:

READ BOOKS TOGETHER. Read fairytales and fables. Read the classics and the modern stories. Read fiction books and books on history. Read them together. Read them aloud. Read them all with equal zeal so there is never any question that books are the portals to imagination, the gateways to new experiences, the windows to other worlds. To *the* world.

Sally Clarkson said, "Introducing our children to rousing tales, great adventures, historical battles, and romantic talks opens children's minds to ponder infinite ideas, dreams, and creative possibilities and to truly enjoy the beauty of learning and growing."[14]

Let us invite our children into our laps and tell them stories of fairies, elves, and dragons, of struggles and overcoming them. Let us write new stories and speak them over their heads at night. Let us pass along the ancient wisdom and universal truths.

Through stories, may we never cease to give children the gift of wonder. The gift of hope.

GO OUTSIDE. Being in nature is going home. The Earth is our true home, after all; our house is merely a shelter. Our bodies and minds weren't meant to live in an indoor, air-conditioned, appliance-humming environment. We've become accustomed to it, for sure. But that's not how we thrive. Instead, find comfort in the sound of swaying trees, and awaken your senses with the sound of rustling leaves.

As Christine Cooper said, "A child's sense of beauty grows from early contact with nature, and his life cannot be fully blessed without this sense. Without it, he is unable to appreciate in future years pure art, and many of the thoughts of great writers, particularly of our poets. Nature's influence on the works and lives of many great men, again, shows us the importance of this study."[15]

Some people assume Wild + Free homeschoolers simply run through fields and splash in puddles all day without a mention of math or a hint of history. But "real learning" doesn't only happen in classrooms. It happens indoors, outdoors, and without doors. It happens in the long spans of time where measuring sticks don't exist and sticks and stones create the building blocks of their education.

So if you're homeschooling, go outside and learn. If your kids are in school, use the precious after-school hours to get outside and learn. Experience the wonder the world has to offer.

STAY CURIOUS. You might think it sounds preposterous to say that parents are the reason our children stop being curious. I mean, what mother or father says to a child, "Stop being curious"?

But that's exactly what we do when we tell children to sit still, stop moving, or pay attention. It's what we do when we tell them not to make a mess with the Play-Doh or scold them for spilling the orange juice. It's what we do when we buy them too many toys or make them stay on the artificial playground surface at the park. It's what we do when we do things for them because it's easier than "fixing" their mistakes. Ah, mistakes. They are, as James Joyce wrote, "the portals of discovery."[16]

We are tired, and curiosity is just too untidy. But being curious always leads to wonder. We don't have to drum up elaborate ideas to foster curiosity; we need only to facilitate it. Our children will lead the way.

In a *New York Times* article, Columbia physics professor Brian Greene wrote, "From the time we can walk and talk, we want to know what things are and how they work—we begin life as little scientists."[17]

Curiosity looks like exploration. It comes in the form of questions and wandering away from the proven methods. It's found off the beaten path and in unfamiliar places. It can be loud and obtrusive, and it can feel uncomfortable at times.

You'll know it when you encounter it because it will interfere with your perfectly planned day. But allow your days to be beautifully inconvenienced. Swing wide those doors to the world.

WELCOME BOREDOM. In the long, drawn-out spans of time, we find the wonder of stillness. If only we could be content with ourselves long enough to make it through the desert of boredom into the oasis of imagination and creativity. If only we could stop convincing ourselves we don't have the resources.

Today, children's boredom muscles are weak. They've atrophied from years of disuse.

Don't mistake their cries of boredom as pain from which they need to be rescued. They are merely the pangs of great ideas about to be born. Don't mistake inactivity as laziness. If we want boredom to do the work of wonder, we must give it time. Don't allow the worry of seeing a child "do nothing" conjure up guilt and self-condemnation. They can only go through the boredom, never around it.

In his brilliant essay "In Praise of Idleness," Bertrand Russell wrote, "It will be said that, while a little leisure is pleasant, men would not know how to fill their days if they had only four hours of work out of the twenty-four. In so far as this is true in the modern world, it is a condemnation of our civilization; it

Here are some ways to help strengthen your children's boredom muscles:

- Spend short increments of time without devices or screens.

- Prepare invitations to discovery, like a table with art supplies or loose objects. (Maybe they'll try them; maybe they won't. But they can't say there was nothing to do.)

- Designate a time to do individual endeavors and then demonstrate things they can do, like read a book, work on a handcraft, or go outside and climb a tree.

- Cultivate a rhythm that includes free time intermixed with activity, so they know they aren't "on their own" for too long.

would not have been true at an earlier period. There was formerly a capacity for light-heartedness and play which has been to some extent inhibited by the cult of efficiency. The modern man thinks that everything ought to be done for the sake of something else, and never for its own sake."[18]

In light of Russell's essay being written in 1932, I can't help but lament that his words fell on deaf ears. Here we are in the twenty-first century, worse for the wear. Not only did the idea of idleness and leisure not catch on, but boredom has been even further banished to the garbage heap, along with Einstein's "holy curiosity" and reading for pleasure.

Maybe we could try again. Maybe we'll see writers and painters, graphic designers and musicians, scientists and doctors emerge from the haze of overwhelm and exhaustion. Maybe we'll see a generation of more contented, happy, creative thinkers.

Maybe, just maybe.

A Call to Wonder

Wonder exists whether we foster it or not. It lives in the depths of our children's souls, and if the embers haven't entirely been snuffed out, it doesn't take much to reawaken the flames.

Sally Clarkson wrote, "Exposing my children to a vast smorgasbord of culture expressed through art, music, theater, architecture, history, and travel was one of the most profoundly influential foundations for their intellect, faith, and engagement in academics."[19]

As parents, we get to stoke our children's natural sense of wonder to discover new things and, in turn, fill them with even more wonder. Connection over correction. Play over programs. Rhythm over regulation. Stories over soapboxes. Curiosity over curriculum. Woods over worksheets.

Wonder is the spark of learning. A child's desire to learn cannot be fanned into flame without it. The good news is that our children are born with all the wonder they will ever need. Our job is not to snuff it out.

Dear parents, you and I have the power to stand in the gap between this world and our children's wonder. We are the wonder seekers, the peacemakers, the passion keepers.

We are the protectors, the preservers, the dark-of-night prayers.

We are the dreamers, the believers, the dare-to-changers.

We are the awakeners of wonder.

8

TO ADVENTURE TOGETHER

If you think adventure is dangerous,
try routine—it's lethal.

—PAULO COELHO

Most families have a favorite TV show. For the past few years, we've alternated between *Shark Tank*, *The Mandalorian*, and reruns of *The Andy Griffith Show*. But once, during a dry spell, we dabbled in a reality show on Animal Planet called *Finding Bigfoot*, which has long since been canceled.

It's about a group of researchers from the Bigfoot Field Researchers Organization (BFRO) who travel to places where Bigfoot sightings are common and conduct investigations in hopes of proving that the creature really does exist. (Some critics dubbed it *Never Finding Bigfoot* because the show's researchers, Ranae, Matt, Cliff, and Bobo, never had any success.)

Despite my reluctance to raise a brood of conspiracy theorists, I let my children watch the show, and they quickly became enthusiasts. (I blame my husband.) I remained the family skeptic but couldn't help but get drawn into their stories and research.

Apparently, there are two schools of thought when it comes to Sasquatch: the paranormalists, who liken it to UFOs, the Loch Ness Monster, and the Abominable Snowman, and the naturalists, who believe there is an elusive species of primate or ape hiding in the deep woods of North America, much like the black rhino in Africa and the giant beaver in Canada.

The TV show took the naturalistic view and attempted to find the creature using thermal imaging equipment, night vision goggles, sound recorders, trail cameras, and eyewitness accounts.

The prospect of such a creature existing in the wild fascinated my kids for a time. Whenever they played in the backyard, I often heard them howling into the wind and smacking branches against the sides of trees to emulate the sound of "wood knocks."

My eldest son, Wyatt, took a more academic approach to deepening this newfound interest. He read all the reports of nearby sightings on the BFRO website[1] and, much to the chagrin of this living-book-loving mama, began purchasing books about cryptozoology, the study of unproven species of animals.

My husband Ben decided he could foster a deeper connection with Wyatt by taking him on an actual BFRO expedition. The organization offers quite a few excursions throughout the year led by experienced guides to remote locations that have generated some kind of reported activity.

The missions are always secret. In fact, Ben had to sign a

nondisclosure agreement about the tactics and location of the trip before they could go. This one happened to be in the southern mountains of Ohio, which is as much as I can tell you for fear of having agents in black suits show up at my door. My two guys passed the phone interview and were welcomed onto the team.

When June finally rolled around, they made their way to the remote camp, leaving me behind with the younger children, not knowing if Wyatt and Ben would ever return to the homestead.

Ben had purchased a thermal imager (or "therm," as they call it) for Wyatt, which would allow him to see "heat signatures" in the dark. These are the shapes of figures that emit body heat, such as humans, bears, squirrels, birds, and, of course, Bigfoot. On the first night of the expedition, Ben and Wyatt were sitting on top of a mountain beside an old logging road with a team of investigators. Wyatt had been scanning the tree line all around them with his therm for about ten minutes, looking for "Squatch," when he suddenly announced that he had spotted one.

Ben was horrified. He hissed at Wyatt to stay quiet, to leave it to the professionals. But Wyatt wouldn't relent. He kept staring through the monocle into the brush, insisting that there was one standing behind a tree looking back at them. Ben finally  grabbed the therm and scanned the tree line. Sure enough, Ben said, there was a figure resembling a bigfoot nearly twenty yards away.

(Now would be a good time to consider whether the BFRO would actually con their own guests with manufactured sightings. But knowing how trigger-happy some Bigfoot enthusiasts can be, one could argue that donning a hairy costume would be a very risky venture, to say the least.)

At this point, the other investigators whipped out their thermal imagers and night vision goggles and followed Wyatt's line of sight into the woods.

"Well, I'll be darned," they said. "You've got one."

They turned on the sound recorders and switched on their headlamps with red bulbs, which apparently don't frighten the big fellas. For the next ten minutes, they heard wood knocks, howls, and brush crunching underfoot, until the noises finally stopped and the heat signature disappeared.

Wyatt and Ben climbed into their sleeping bags in the early morning, with adrenaline surging through their veins and their hearts pounding out of their chests, but still not entirely convinced of what they had seen. But the next day, the investigators went to the site and found ten fifteen-inch footprints in the mud. An embedded reporter from *Popular Mechanics* magazine even documented the excursion.[2]

For the rest of the weekend, Ben was identified by the group as "Wyatt's dad." Wyatt was heralded for his keen observational skills and ability to remain calm under pressure. They even gave him an award: a replica of the footprint cast from the famous Patterson-Gimlin sighting, which was filmed in Bluff Creek, California, in 1967. (You'd probably recognize the footage if you saw it.)

Ben and Wyatt would never go so far as to say that what they saw was actually Bigfoot. But what they discovered out there on an undisclosed mountaintop in godforsaken Ohio was something that could never be found in a cul-de-sac basketball game or a bounce house at a local strip mall: Risk. Excitement. And an unforgettable adventure for father and son.

Getting Outside

Adventure starts with getting outside. If getting outside sounds complicated, it's because we make it so. The solution is not to think about it. It's to go. First thing. Before breakfast. Before everyone's dressed. Before you change your mind.

Long ago, when I was homeschooling three little boys, I dreamed of mornings filled with poetry readings, conversations, and creative writing. But a babe on my hip made it impossible to sit.

We couldn't make it through a book without someone breaking down. We couldn't construct a handcraft when my hands were too occupied to be of assistance.

So we went outdoors.

We didn't go far, mind you. Sometimes we only made it out the front door. We splashed in puddles and danced in the rain. We drew on sidewalks and made pies out of mud. We counted shells and skipped rocks and made shapes in the clouds. We built forts out of branches and learned to climb trees.

I used to think I had to plan, pack, and make provisions to go outdoors. But nature doesn't send us an invitation with a list of requirements. It simply beckons us to come. Just as we are, with whatever we have. It's always there, always waiting, and always ready to teach us another lesson.

In those early days of being home with my boys, we never found our rhythm sitting still and learning indoors. Instead, we found our peace in the presence of wonder and wild things.

We went outdoors in desperation but found more than a place to run wild and free. We found the greatest classroom we could ever hope to know.

We found contentment in the summer breezes and the sundry shades of autumn leaves. We watched butterflies and dragonflies and the flight of bumblebees. We learned the songs of all our backyard birds and the sound of swaying trees. We discovered that wonder existed whether we chased it or not, but life became one continuous wonder when we followed its lead.

Nature isn't the only place to find adventure, but adventuring together in nature is a wonderful way to show—not just tell—our kids the importance of doing hard things. Because, let's face it, nature can get hairy and uncomfortable. There's bad weather and pesky insects, let alone physical effort. Hearing "I'm hot" or "I'm itchy" one too many times is a sure way to make parents want to throw in the towel. Not every family is a camping family or even a hiking family. But giving our kids the chance to flex their adventure muscles in different ways can teach them lessons we could never express with words.

My friend and fellow Wild + Free mama Greta Eskridge wrote a book about adventuring together as a family. She shared, "When we embark on a hard adventure with our kids, we must make sure our kids know we believe in them. This not only helps them to believe in their own ability to conquer the challenge but also knits their hearts with ours as we rise to the challenge together."[3]

Whether it's summiting a mountain or riding a Jet Ski for the first time, spending time outdoors builds confidence and brings you just a little bit closer to one another with each encounter.

Let's trade those screens for panoramic scenes of trees and mountains and stars. Let's open the doors and let the children outside. Let's let them move, climb trees, skip rocks, make believe, build hideouts in hollows, and find treasures on the seashore.

Let's take them back to the place where they belong.

The Gift of Adventure

My friend Andrea Pratt and her husband Andrew decided to change how their family celebrated Christmas each year.

"In the early years of navigating Christmas and birthdays with children, I was caught off guard by my family's generosity of gifts and the emotions it would bring," Andrea said. "It felt a little like dread, a little like bewilderment, and a lot like stress. The dust storm of gift wrap would settle and all I saw was stuff I did not know what to do with. It was not just me. I will never forget one Christmas when my three-year-old daughter melted in a puddle of despair at the realization there were more unopened gifts. This was an opportunity to do something different."

They decided, from that moment on, to give their children experiences, rather than presents.

Andrea and Andrew came up with ideas for more enriching gifts and invited their family members to do the same: things like zoo memberships, gymnastics classes, and tickets to *The Nutcracker*. These simple changes helped reduce the sense of dread, but they knew there was more they could do.

They realized they could give the gift of adventure.

Now, on Christmas morning, their kids wake up with the same sense of anticipation as any other child, but their presents contain clues about where their next adventure will take them. Andrew even devises a scavenger hunt with assignments, such as climbing a tree and using a compass. The search eventually leads to a password that unlocks a PowerPoint presentation, which reveals the big adventure.

They always leave the day after Christmas, so the kids don't have to wait very long to enjoy the adventure.

The Pratts let their extended family members know they can

give the children gifts but encourage them to make their gifts part of the experience, such as spending money, hotel rooms, or books for the trip.

A few years ago, the Pratts took their kids dogsledding in the frozen plains of Minnesota. They found one of the only dog-sledding outfits that doesn't have an age limit, a company called Chilly Dogs Sled Dog Trips, so all the Pratt kids—two, four, and seven at the time—could join in the adventure.

Andrea said, "We stuffed stockings with consumables, wrapped dogsledding books, and outfitted the children with new gear for the trip. To add to the mystery, we planned a scavenger hunt with tasks that would earn letters, which formed a password unveiling a slideshow of our trip."

When they arrived, the family met the owners, staff, and other guests in a cozy room with a roaring fire. They were given some history and instructions before heading out to meet the dogs.

Their sleds were pulled by teams of Alaskan huskies, some of whom had actually run the 938-mile Iditarod race in Alaska. These were not pets or rescue animals but athletes that loved having a job to do.

Andrea said, "In a matter of moments, we were in the woods on an open trail without a single sound other than the gentle swish of the sled atop fresh powder. It was shocking how quiet it was in this north-country wilderness. The tree branches were heavy with snow and the sun glistened across the open trail ahead of us. It was both beautiful and exhilarating."

It was a rather cold outing, as you might imagine, and any experience with young children is going to come with some hardship, but this is one the Pratt children will never forget.

Andrea said, "Choosing to live a life of creating experiences with small children requires a certain amount of grit and determination. More often than not, there are obstacles in between your family and the goal you have. But these obstacles are often what brings out a necessary fight from within. A fight that your children need to see. Perfection is unattainable, but perseverance is essential in this life."

Andrea said she realizes now that it was never really dread that she felt in those early years but rather a longing for a deeper connection with her family. Now, when her family recalls their adventures, they laugh about all the wonderful parts, and the difficult ones seem to have faded away.

"We have a connecting thread to a time when we experienced something new together, something we worked and fought for," Andrea said. "True connection. Shouldn't that be the goal of every gift?"

So set your course accordingly and brace yourself, dear friend, because a vision worth following is never an easy one. "Life is either a daring adventure," as Helen Keller said, "or nothing."[4]

Fifty-Two Family Hikes

After moving to southern Oregon from New Mexico a few years ago, my friend Lindsay Rowe and her family wanted to take in all the beautiful sights of their new home. So they set the audacious goal of completing fifty-two family hikes during the first year.

They searched for hiking trails within a two-hour drive so they could take a picnic and make it an easy day trip for their two youngest children, who were eight and four at the time. As it turned out, there were so many hiking locations in southern Oregon that they couldn't get to even half of them.

"In the beginning, I wanted to create something to keep their focus and help them notice tiny details on our hikes,"

Lindsay said. "I challenged each of us to find a heart on each hike, and we always did. It didn't matter if it was a rock, a leaf, on tree bark, or on a bug. I documented every heart, and we took a selfie on each hike. Still to this day my kids will find hearts for me everywhere we go."

On one hike, they spotted a great horned owl fly across the trail ahead and land in a tree on the switchback below. They quickly followed in search of it until, at last, they saw where it had landed.

"We stood still barely breathing as we watched it turn its head and hoot," Lindsay said. "It was one of those magical moments that we never wanted to end, so we stayed in one spot for as long as our kids would let us. They stood quiet for a very long time with their little wide eyes watching that magnificent bird. When we got home, we drew that owl in our nature journals, so we'd never forget it."

There were times when they got caught in the rain. Times where the kids weren't too thrilled about hiking. And times when they would have preferred to do anything else.

But in the end, embarking upon fifty-two family hikes brought them closer as a family. They learned how to empathize when someone was feeling worn out. They learned how to slow down and comfort each other. And they learned how to lift each other's spirits by singing, making up games, telling stories, and whistling.

"We took all the things we learned about nature observation and kept our study closer to home as we bought ourselves a little farm to settle down. That year of hikes set our family up with a treasure chest of memories and taught us how to really *see* the beautiful world around us. We'll never forget it."

Our great opportunity as wild and free families is to embrace adventure as a way of life.

Learning from Adventure

I would like to believe that everything my children need to learn, they can learn from books. And while it's true that books are portals to incredible places and worlds we may never travel to, kids need to experience some of these places firsthand. There is simply no substitute for experience.

When we study early American history, I can read a hundred books on Jamestown and the Revolutionary War, or I can pack up the car and drive them to a nearby historical site where they can dip candles, dye clothes, walk the cobbled streets, and explore replicas of the early dwellings.

Kids, as it turns out, don't have any trouble learning about things they're interested in. If you give them a choice between studying a topic or experiencing it for themselves, experience wins every time. Adventure is such a powerful teacher that once you've done it, it's hard to learn any other way.

Often, the biggest obstacle between our kids and adventure is us. Adventure runs counter to everything we stand for as adults. Our mental hard drives have been reformatted from years of domestication and "maturity" to prioritize work and efficiency above all else. Our schedules are filled with only "important stuff," leaving no time for frivolous activity.

However, kids need adventure in their everyday lives. Not just once-in-a-lifetime trips to enjoy the spectacular as a spectator—although those are wonderful too—but real experiences, ordinary ones that jump-start their imaginations and foster connection with the world around them. Ones that leave them dirty, wet, and tired. Ones they can have outside their backdoor each day.

My husband and I are always looking for ways to help our children learn from experiences. We travel to as many places as we can; fuel their creative interests with books and crafts, building materials and manuals, software and tools; and explain the inner workings of our companies so they better understand how organizations work.

But nothing compares to the experience of living learning.

We were able to give Wyatt a taste of this a few years ago. We had been following the Instagram account of Fell & Fair for some time, which features inspiring photos of young adults reenacting scenes from mythical lore and medieval history.[5]

The founder of Fell & Fair, Zan Campbell, grew up homeschooled by a mother who read the works of J. R. R. Tolkien and C. S. Lewis to him and his siblings. Even after a career as a navy helicopter pilot, Zan never lost his passion for imagining new worlds, battling the forces of evil, and creating costumes.

So when Zan announced an immersive event called "Weekend Warrior" and invited guests to dress up like knights and fight each other using authentic-looking foam weaponry, Ben booked two tickets.

He and Wyatt traveled to South Carolina on a crisp October weekend, not knowing what to expect. They came upon nearly two hundred adults dressed in tunics, chain mail, and even full suits of armor, each of them brandishing weapons that looked to be straight out of an episode of *Game of Thrones*.

There were four factions set to battle each other: the Sea Lords, the Kingsmen, the Rangers, and the Hearth-guard. All were warned by their leaders to carry weapons at all times and to expect anything.

On that first night, tensions mounted at their feast in the mead hall and carried over to the one-on-one battles in the arena. By the time the first battle broke out the next morning, everyone was on edge.

Ben and Wyatt helped form a "shield wall" with the rest of the Rangers, just as they had been instructed, while their archers flanked the Kingsmen who confronted them on the main road. For the next thirty minutes, they fended off polearms being jabbed at them, battle axes being swung at their limbs, swords slicing through the air, and arrows zipping past their heads.

The leaders of the factions never broke character, which gave each player a taste of what it would have been like in actual battle. Hooded spies from other factions darted between trees and carried out secret missions at night. The sound of a war cry from the Hearth-guard's campsite and the music of a fiddle player in the town square gave the whole experience a sense of authenticity.

Ben always tells Wyatt that if he doesn't like these strange excursions, they can always leave. In fact, when it involves primitive camping, Ben always hopes Wyatt will want to leave early, but he never does. In fact, when it started pouring rain on the final day of Weekend Warrior, Wyatt suited up for battle.

There is learning about medieval culture, and then there is experiencing it. Living it. *Feeling* it.

Reading a book about medieval history is benign. You can try to understand the culture, the food, the battles, and the politics from the words on a page, but fiefdom doesn't make sense until you have to serve a king of your own.

Adventure as a Way of Life

It's never too late to make adventure a core value of your family. Just as we work to build connection, communication, and wonder into our family culture, we can make room for regular adventure.

Start by holding a family meeting. Tell everyone that from this day forward, you will be a family that adventures together. Ask everyone to share something they'd love to do, crazy or not. And then figure out a way to make it happen.

Maybe you don't feel adventurous. Maybe you have an aversion to risk. You've got a job to do. A family to protect. Mouths to feed. Maybe you've been burned before by taking a chance.

Listen, you don't have to climb Mount Everest or go BASE jumping. Adventure is shaking loose the conventions of everyday life and doing something that makes life more meaningful.

You may not have weekdays. You may not even have weekends. You may have obligations between nine and five. But let me remind you that what happens between five and nine is totally up to you.

If you have little children at home, it's great to start making adventure a habit when they are young. Create scavenger hunts and obstacle courses in your backyard. Go to museums and new cities or become tourists in your own town. Get outside, get wet, and camp under the stars. And don't, whatever you do, stop as they get older.

Our teens might outgrow the activities of childhood, but they want adventure all the same. They crave autonomy and a distinction from their younger selves, so we must find new ways to engage their wild hearts and give them the risk and sense of danger that makes them feel alive.

But it's important for them to have their own adventures too. Allow them to take risks and build a life of adventure through their imaginations and explorations of the world around them. In a world where adults are trying to remove all risk from childhood, we must hold the line.

Writer Roald Dahl said, "The more risks you allow your children to take, the better they learn how to take care of themselves."[6]

Travel every chance you get. Overnight trips, long weekends, overseas travel, or a monthlong cross-country trip in an RV—it doesn't matter. Just go. Having kids is a reason *to* travel, never a reason to stay home.

In the end, it isn't really about the *what* but the *who* and *why* we adventure. And really, what is this life if not an opportunity to create your own adventure?

Maybe you're not going to go on a secret Sasquatch expedition anytime soon. But I hope you're inspired to embark on your own big, wild, and hairy adventure. Discover what your family loves to do outside the box. Find your own Bigfoot.

Choose Your Own Adventure

One of my favorite children's book authors is Jan Brett. Her beautiful Nordic-themed illustrations and enchanting story lines have enthralled my kids ever since they could sit upright.

But my favorite part of her books is the sidebars. Alongside the main illustrations on each page are smaller drawings that foreshadow what's coming next. I have resisted pointing these out to my kids, lest I ruin for them the joy of discovering them on their own, but they hint at an adventure that's coming next.

Yes, we all have responsibilities. We all have duties and obligations. But we can tuck adventures into the sidebars of everyday life and make the most of our precious time together.

If you don't like the course your life is on, you can reroute it.

If you don't like the narrative you're living, you can rewrite it.

If you don't like the formula you've been prescribed, you can create your own.

Our children get their cues about what is reasonable to pursue in life from us. If we play it safe, so will they. If we act frightened and take no chances, neither will they. We are their assigned adventure guides, and like it or not, we are the ones who decide whether they get to take the scenic route.

By our lifestyle, we either encourage our children to dream big and dare greatly or let them know that adventure is meant for extreme athletes and bygone explorers of the world.

Society has its own ideas for what's reasonable for your family. It offers predetermined work hours, predesigned housing arrangements, and predefined lifestyles for you to embrace. It's just waiting for you to accept the terms of agreement.

But it doesn't have to be that way. You can decide what's reasonable for your family.

Adventure is waiting for those who seek it. Change the kind of vacations you take. Alter how you spend your nights and weekends. Because if we don't foster adventure in our children's lives, they'll find it elsewhere. (All those kids playing Fortnite wouldn't be doing so if their real lives were adventurous.) Our great opportunity as wild and free families is to embrace adventure as a way of life.

If you want to raise explorers of the wild, you have to be one yourself.

Get outside. Get dirty.

Start oohing and ahhing.

Begin wondering and wandering again.

Be afraid. Be adventurous.

If you lead the way, before you know it, your children will be leading you.

9

TO UNLEASH
THEIR GIFTS

*Kids deserve the right to think
that they can change the world.*

—LOIS LOWRY

As wild and free families, we believe in giving ourselves and our children the freedom to flourish in our gifts and passions. We actively look for the strengths in each other and try to fan those into flame.

We're careful to never put any child in a box. Many of us know what it's like to grow up as "the athletic one," "the smart one," or "the handy one." You feel like you can't venture outside your assigned role in life, and it makes your siblings feel like they'll never be as good as you in that area. Or maybe you grew up with the stigma of "not being good at anything," which is even worse.

When our kids show signs of excelling in a particular field, we try to fuel their gifts by offering encouraging words, giving them the opportunity to spend more time in that area, and making sure they have the resources they need. In our family, we call these resources "tools of creations." We've told our kids that if they have an interest that aligns with their gifts, we'll do our best to provide the necessary resources to pursue it.

Over the years, we've procured secondhand sewing machines, old field recorders and microphones, screenwriting software, art supplies, podcasting equipment, and silicone mold-making kits, and we've borrowed string instruments, tool sets, and green-screen backdrops, among many other things.

We can't always afford everything they want, and we don't buy everything we can. There has to be a dedicated season of working on the craft to prove their commitment before we purchase anything. And it has to fall in the category of creating something, rather than merely consuming media. Not every request is approved, and not everything we greenlight turns into something. But we believe in fueling our children's gifts. Children cannot possibly know what they're good at without trying it.

Isn't this the way filmmakers start out? Someone gives them a camcorder and plenty of time to use it. Isn't this the way astronomers get started? Someone buys them a telescope and points it at the sky.

Just as great thinkers, writers, mathematicians, and philosophers need copious amounts of time, supplies, and spaces to practice their craft, so do engineers, mechanics, and artists. Imagine the impact you could make on the world through your children by simply investing in their interests and talents.

Here's to "Useless" Dreams

My daughter Annie was drawing at the kitchen table the other day—probably unicorns or the likenesses of our family members with, of course, a pet unicorn—when she suddenly looked up at me.

"I want to be a church man when I grow up," she said. "Can girls be church mans? Because I want to hold the book and marry people."

She looked off in the distance and thought about it some more.

"I either want to be a cowgirl or a church man when I grow up," she continued. "But horses are expensive, so I don't know about a cowgirl. I think I'll be a church man."

Our children grow up with very little awareness of the impossibilities or impracticalities of life. Those doubts and fears make their way into their precious little minds through the careless remarks of naysayers or the biases that are reflected in society, media, and culture. Without these negative influences, our children awaken each day with heads full of possibility and hearts full of courage.

This is why the family is so important. It's meant to be an incubator for the hopes and dreams of children, a safe haven for wondering and wandering. Our kids come into the world trying to figure out their identities. They become aware of their shortcomings, thanks to the candor of fellow middle school students and the harsh commentary of social media. But they often struggle to know what makes them exceptional in the world. Far too often, children's dreams become fashioned into a construct that reduces risk, crushes creativity, and eradicates idealism.

This is why I stopped letting my children watch *Thomas the Tank Engine & Friends* when they were little. Sir Topham Hatt's remarks to the trains as being "useful engines" were a blight on childhood wonder. The term "useful" is brandished by the railway director like a weapon; he uses it to punish the engines that don't behave properly and to reward those that do exactly what they're supposed to do.

For example, on a drizzly day in Sodor, an engine named Henry refuses to come out of his tunnel for fear that the rain will ruin his lovely green paint and red stripes. Sir Topham Hatt warns him to get back to work or "we shall take away your rails, and leave you here for always and always."[1]

When Henry still refuses to come out, the railway employees block the engine in his tunnel, and his friends pass him, one by one, expressing their displeasure. Henry is left alone, wondering if he'll ever work again. The episode ends with the narrator saying, "I think he deserved his punishment, don't you?"

"Useful" is an important concept for marketplace ventures and for anyone seeking employment with a company that has a specific job to do. But who says our children can't make up their own rules? Can't disrupt industries with their innovative thinking? Can't define their own "usefulness"?

"Useful" is a subjective term and one on which every parent should withhold judgment until the fruits of our children's endeavors are made evident. After all, a degree in math or science, or any of the fields considered to be practical, does not guarantee success. And what is success, after all?

Your family was designed to protect the dreams of your children. You are meant to be the Medici for your young artists, idealists, and dreamers, nurturing their notions and fanning their gifts into flame.

People will always say it can't be done until finally someone does it. Perhaps that someone will be your child. Why can't it be your child?

Our role as parents is to unleash our children's gifts and provide them with opportunities to work out their ideas, no matter how impractical or useless they might appear. There is plenty of time for course correction. Mistakes are not life sentences. Miscalculations are learning opportunities.

It's up to the future to determine which ideas will pan out and which ones won't.

As parents, that's not our job.

Our job is to call out the best in our children.

To believe in them.

To walk alongside them, even when we don't know where the path will lead.

I think—in fact, I know—we'll be amazed.

Creating the Future World

When I think about the kind of world that I want my children to be a part of—the world they will create—I want it to be one that welcomes their highest ambitions and most peculiar passions. I want a world with compassion, kindness, constructive problem-solving, and creative thinking. A world where they are not bound by the limitations of society, but rather released by the dreams in their hearts and the ideas in their heads. A world where they are free to feel, free to think, and free to be.

No one ever grows up dreaming of working in a cubicle. No one believes the highest expression of their lives will be the company picnic. These are young Picassos, Edisons, Goodalls, and Ginsburgs we are raising, if only we will see them for the potential each of them possesses.

This brave new world doesn't start when our children leave the nest. It begins right now in the little universe that is our family, our household. We are responsible for the microecosystems that birth their dreams, their character, their feelings, their opportunities, and their beliefs about the world. We get to nurture the environment that births the world-changers of the future.

Here are several ways we can begin to unleash our children's gifts.

UNDERSTAND THEIR EMOTIONS

My five-year-old, Millie, is a sensitive sort. Whenever we're on a long road trip and the kids are watching a movie in the back seat, I'll glance in the rearview mirror at just the right moment and watch the tears welling up in her heterochromatic eyes (she's got one blue eye and one green one).

If I call attention to her tears—ask her if she needs a tissue—she quickly wipes them away with her chubby, little hands and says, "I don't know why I'm crying."

Oh, I do, my poor, sweet Millie. I do.

My girl feels deeply. And as her mother, I am committed to helping her understand that her emotions are a superpower. I want her to know that her feelings are a strength, not a weakness.

Many of us grew up in homes or went to schools where expressing emotion was considered a weakness. This is one of the great tragedies of childhood.

In his remarkable and eye-opening book *Simplicity Parenting*, Kim John Payne wrote, "Long after babies are weaned from the breast or bottle, they continue to nurse from their parents' emotions. . . . Children feed off their parents' emotions."[2]

Not every adult is comfortable with emotion. But it is not our children's job to make *us* feel comfortable with their emotions. It is our job to make *them* feel comfortable and accepted. After all, we *are* our emotions. Every neuron in our brain, every fiber in our being, is dictated by our emotions.

If we hope to hold on to our relationship with our kids and unleash their potential in this world, we have to become more comfortable with their emotions. And even if we can't—even if we've somehow grown calloused from our own torrid experiences—we can at least change how we *respond* to our kids.

In his book *Permission to Feel*, Marc Brackett, founder of the Yale Center for Emotional Intelligence, wrote, "Because of their still developing vocabularies and powers of communication, we need to listen extra closely to our children if we're interested in knowing what they feel and why. We need to make sure they understand that we welcome hearing what happens in their lives—the good and the bad, the happy and the sad, the successes and the failures."[3]

The challenge of parenting is that our children often reveal emotions about us that we may not always want to hear. Brackett continued: "It's scary to hear other people express their feelings, because we may have to accept some hard truths about ourselves. And in response, we may feel obliged to take some action—even to change, which is usually the last thing we want to do."[4] We hear a judgment about us when all they want is to feel without judgment.

Another challenge is that when we allow our children to feel and express emotion, we worry that it will be messy and out of control. But the goal isn't simply to become emotional people, tossing our feelings all over each other. The goal is to get comfortable with our emotions, to better understand our emotions, to learn through our emotions, and, ultimately, to regulate our emotions.

No one ever talks about emotional regulation. I didn't understand much about it until a few years ago. But it's a balancing act that occurs within us from the time we are in our mother's womb. We begin regulating our emotions from her heartbeat, the flow of her movement, and the sound of her voice.

Babies want to suckle—be it a breast, a bottle, or a thumb—because it offers emotional comfort. This is why babies sleep better on your chest, listening to your heartbeat and breathing. It's why they cry out for comfort in the night, seeking co-regulation.

Humans regulate off each other: parent to child, child to parent, and adult to adult. It's why someone's bad mood can alter the state of another and why joy and laughter are contagious.[5]

If we are going to help our children become healthy adults, we have to help them understand their emotions and the all-important skill of self-regulation. (Some of us might have to learn those skills ourselves before we can show our kids what healthy self-regulation looks like.)

It's in our facial expressions, our tone of voice, our body language, and other nonverbal signals. It's understanding the source of our feelings and determining how they are influencing our current reality. And it's learning to regulate our emotions, rather than letting them control us.

Gaining emotion skills is integral to unlocking the potential in our children—and in all of us, really. Some would say that emotional intelligence is more important than IQ or any other measure of success.

If we want our children to succeed, we have to give them the tools to understand themselves and others. To make connections in the world based on healthy interactions. And to grow in knowledge at their own pace, as knowledge fuels those connections and current understanding.

It's not easy to change. It takes practice and more practice.

But we can do it. We were born to do it. And when we do, it will radically impact our children, the future, and the world.

FOSTER THEIR CURIOSITY

When the Mars rover *Perseverance* landed on the rusty planet in 2020, it rekindled a spark of interest in my children for all things space. Well, in them and the rest of the free world.

It's fascinating to think about the years each technological advance has taken to develop. This isn't the first rover to land on Mars. But this time, a helicopter named *Ingenuity* joined *Perseverance*, adding to the breadth of information that NASA scientists will be able to gather about life on Mars.

In celebration of this historic feat, a tweet from former NASA engineer Ben Cichy resurfaced from a year earlier,

 which read: "Got a 2.4 GPA my first semester in college. Thought maybe I wasn't cut out for engineering. Today I've landing two spacecraft on Mars, and designing one for the moon. STEM is hard for everyone. Grades ultimately aren't what matters. Curiosity and persistence matter."[6]

What a testament to the power of curiosity.

But what's interesting to note is that several commenters criticized Cichy's grammar on his tweet, as if he still isn't worthy. (To all the grammar police in the world: please sit down and be quiet. The man helped land two spacecraft on Mars.)

Curiosity is the key to all real learning and will take our children further than textbooks ever could. It is the driving force behind anything that we seek to know and understand.

Of course, we want our children to learn all the things and get the best education possible. But if we truly want our children to be lifelong learners, we have to foster an atmosphere of curiosity.

Here are several ways to foster curiosity in your own home:

1. Be open to mistakes.

2. Explore more, control less.

3. Let your children guide you.

4. Accept messes as part of the process.

5. Ask questions. Don't always be the expert.

As our children get older, let's stay curious. Let's allow our adolescents and teens to be the experts on their own research. Let's not correct their interests or passions right out of them. Let's not "parent" every whimsical idea or dream to death.

Let's see their deep dives down seemingly random rabbit holes as a dress rehearsal for the upcoming show. Let's marvel at the ways their minds are mapping the skills needed to learn new things. Let's find pleasure in the process and remember that all of it is part of this beautiful thing called life.

GIVE THEM DOWNTIME

It's not easy to turn off our brains. There's always a clock, an app, or even a smartwatch communicating with us about the time, the news, or the number of steps we've taken today.

We like to stay busy. We like to be important. We are averse to boredom and allergic to silence. We're workaholics. Workout-aholics. App-aholics. We're glued to our phones, and we can't stop.

Celeste Headlee, author of *Do Nothing: How to Break Away from Overworking, Overdoing, and Underliving*, wrote, "Essentially, we are working our way out of happiness and well-being."[7] And she's right. French mathematician Blaise Pascal famously said, "All of humanity's problems stem from man's inability to sit quietly in a room alone."[8] (If this were Instagram, I'd post a "hands-raised" emoji.)

We've all fought the urge to check our phones. But it's no use. They've got control of us. In his book *The Shallows*, Nicholas Carr pointed to studies showing that the brain rewires itself to recognize our phones as an additional appendage and constantly forces us to think that looking at our phones is the most important thing we can do.[9] In other words, not only do our phones not improve our lives, but they actually diminish our productivity.

We've gradually lost the ability to sit alone with our thoughts, to be okay with inactivity, which is why it is imperative that we, as parents, fight to regain the ancient disciplines of solitude within our own households. The opportunity for downtime is one of the greatest gifts we can offer our children.

All our scrolling, streaming, and surfing has altered the dreams of our children, and it's time we get them back. In 2019, Harris Poll asked three thousand kids, ages eight to twelve, to choose from five professions: astronaut, musician, professional athlete, teacher, or YouTuber. In China, 56 percent of kids made astronaut the top choice. In America, it was YouTuber.[10]

Heaven help us.

Margaret Wise Brown, author of the beloved children's book *Goodnight Moon*, wrote, "In this modern world where activity is stressed almost to the point of mania, quietness as a childhood need is too often overlooked. Yet a child's need for quietness is . . . an essential part of all awareness. In quiet times and sleepy times, a child can dwell in thoughts of his own, and in songs and stories of his own."[11]

While modern systems reward activity, thoughtful parents are opting out. While modern technology amplifies noise, intentional parents are slowly unplugging. Not for everything. Not forever. But for a season, a quiet growing time, as Charlotte Mason called it.[12] While modern culture glorifies chaos, wild and free parents are choosing connection. While modern education makes use of screens and worksheets, enlightened teachers are restoring the lost arts of storybooks and climbing trees. While the masses are simply going through the motions, we are choosing meaningful activities that engage the heart, mind, and soul.

Payne describes downtime as a kind of punctuation that disallows chaotic overactivity, just as a period or comma brings clarity to a sentence. In fact, he prescribes boredom three times a day.[13]

I know, you're too busy for downtime. There are lessons and school programs, grocery runs and homework. But the busier you are, the more downtime you need.

"Idleness is not just a vacation, an indulgence, or a vice; it is as indispensable to the brain as vitamin D is to the body, and deprived of it, we suffer a mental affliction as disfiguring as rickets," essayist Tim Kreider wrote in the *New York Times*.[14]

He continued, "The space and quiet that idleness provides is a necessary condition for standing back from life and seeing it whole, for making unexpected connections and waiting for the wild summer lightning strikes of inspiration—it is, paradoxically, necessary to getting any work done."

By fostering a comfort with quietness when our children are young, we set them up for a life in which they can be content. A life in which silence is not empty but full of new ideas. A life in which stillness doesn't lack focus but holds full awareness. A life from which they can connect, create, and collaborate.

After all, as Payne wrote, "the ordinary allows for the exceptional, but not the reverse."[15]

To all the parents choosing peace and simplicity over being stressed and rushed, to all those seeking wonder and curiosity over checks and boxes—keep going. I see you. Tending the garden of childhood is invisible but important work, and your efforts are not in vain.

I love this other gem by Payne: "Simplification is not just about taking things away. It is about making room, creating space in your life, your intentions, and your heart."[16] By creating more downtime, we are not taking things away from our children; we are giving them more.

Less stress, more savoring.

Less chaos, more creating.

Less spending, more sharing.

Less things, more thoughtfulness.

Less madness, more mindfulness.

BELIEVE IN THEM

In the 2006 movie *The Pursuit of Happyness*, Chris Gardner, portrayed by Will Smith, is playing basketball with his young son, who tells him that he wants to be a professional basketball player when he grows up.

Gardner starts to tell him that he's too short to make it in the NBA, that it's the wrong dream.

And then he stops himself. He pulls himself together and then pulls his son close.

"Don't ever let someone tell you you can't do something. Not even me," he says. "You got a dream, you got to protect it. People can't do something themselves, they want to tell you that you can't do it. You want something, go get it. Period."

Believing that our children can learn and do anything is vital to helping them reach their potential. The realists of the world may argue that it will give them false hope and set them on a futile course that won't end well. They see it as an act of responsibility to advise their children to go the practical route.

But these parents are operating out of a fixed mindset that keeps them doing the same things for years on end with no growth, no potential, and they try to instill these same values in their kids.

In her book *Limitless Mind*, Stanford professor Jo Boaler wrote, "A change from believing there are limits to learning and life to believing that anything can be learned or achieved is a change from a fixed to a growth mindset. When we make this change, it has a transformative effect on our lives. We stop thinking we are not good enough and start to take more risks."[17]

My friend and fellow Wild + Free homeschooler Naomi Ovando inspires me with how she unleashes her children's gifts. All her children have enjoyed helping in the kitchen, but her thirteen-year-old son, Lucas, has loved baking things since he was a little boy. Some days he would make cookies, and other days it would be a cake or bread.

"Watching his eyes light up as he experimented made my mama heart happy," Naomi told me.

Once, Lucas taught himself how to make chocolate and experimented with the ingredients until he was happy. After seeing how much people loved his creations, he started selling them to friends and neighbors.

He used a portion of the proceeds to purchase supplies for the homeless, such as socks, beanies, blankets, and rain ponchos. He handed them out whenever they crossed paths with a person in need.

Naomi said, "I love the quote by J. R. R. Tolkien: 'Even the smallest person can change the course of the future.' One of our family goals is to teach our children to serve others. We frequently tell them that, even as children, they can have an impact on the lives of others. They have a special role to play in this world and can be a blessing to another person. We want to teach them that they are important and significant and that their actions can make a difference."

Believing in our children's potential is one thing. Giving them the time, space, and opportunity to develop their gifts is another. Most of us are too busy trying to find our own way in the world, let alone make space for our children to find theirs too. It's easier to relegate them to the playroom or the schoolroom when we're the ones responsible for paying the bills and putting food on the table.

But supporting our children's gifts is one of the greatest investments we can make. And it's made easier by this wild and free lifestyle of slowing time down and giving them space to experiment.

"As wild and free families, we have the freedom to give our children the time and space to create and make," Naomi said. "We also have the freedom to make time for things that matter most to us. I know I don't get it all right, and I often worry that I'm not doing enough. But when I see our children's creativity and their love and compassion toward others, I know that we're doing something right by slowing down."

When our children are grown and gone, when they're chasing after their dreams and reaching for the stars, I want to be able to look back and see that I was standing on the right side of history. I want to look back and know that I championed everything they endeavored to do. That I didn't believe they would be held back by their challenges and limitations. And that I perhaps whispered the encouragement they needed to hear to be able to go out and change the world.

The world already has plenty of naysayers. What our children need are those who will tell them they can.

10

TO UNLOCK
THEIR POTENTIAL

Motherhood is about raising and
celebrating the child you have,
not the child you thought you would have.

—JOAN RYAN

.

Our babies come into this world with a mix of
preparation and prayer, a comingling of mortality
and the miraculous. We count their fingers and
toes and breathe a sigh of relief when we get to ten.
We wait for the okay from the doctors and go home to begin
the work of keeping this tiny precious human alive. Feeding.
Burping. Swaddling. Rocking. Sleeping. Repeat.

Our days and nights are consumed with the task of meeting
needs and needing sleep all at once. If all goes well, we bond
with our babies and eventually find a rhythm that helps us
survive—thrive even.

The pediatricians ask about milestones. Smiling. Rolling
over. Sitting up. Crawling. Speaking those first words.

We know there are ranges of "normal," but we still worry when they don't hit the markers as quickly as their peers. Eventually they find their way. We find ours. And we breathe another sigh of relief.

We don't stop to wonder why they only crawl with one side of their body. Why they hate being on their tummies. Or why they start walking before they even crawl.

We call them cute. Quirky. Overachievers.

We know that our babies are unique, and their movement is just another way they are becoming their own person. What we don't realize—we're never told—is that the movements of a child, from the time they are in utero to when they are walking, are directly related to their neurology.

Did you know that 50 percent of everything a person will ever know is learned in the first year of life?

This isn't due to the information we put in but to the natural development a baby's brain undergoes through movement. That's pretty incredible. A baby's brain is literally wired for brilliance, and it's never too late to restore what has been lost and reclaim the potential of each and every child.

The story of my family would not be complete without an account of my youngest son's remarkable journey. Gifted with a divergent mind, Cody is the first to engineer creative solutions to common household problems and to look after the well-being of his little sisters.

What could have been regarded as a neurological obstacle has been used to unlock his mind's greatest potential. My hope is that our story will encourage you to see the possibilities within your own children . . . and even within you.

A Beautiful Mind

I stood behind my six-and-a-half-year-old son as he played with wooden letters at the table. This was the third year in a row we were practicing the alphabet. He picked up on most things rather quickly, but when it came to reading and writing, each day was like starting all over again.

Cody was a complex child, reckless in some ways but calculated in others. He never pushed my buttons but constantly caused me to question what he was thinking. He did fearless things like climb the kitchen cabinets and scale the sides of his crib at ten months old.

He started crawling around six months and was walking by eight months. He had incredible coordination, rarely stumbled, and never fell. He could also focus intently on mechanisms. One day, before he could even talk, we discovered that he had unscrewed all the outlet plates in the house.

He was always doing something, from dribbling a basketball with our teenage neighbor to playing his heart out on a set of drums. One morning, when he was only two and a half, I found him in the kitchen making breakfast. There were raw cracked eggs on the counter, on the floor, and dripping out of the refrigerator door. But there he was, sitting on the counter with three raw eggs in a pan on the stove. Never mind that he had already made a cup of coffee and brought it to my mother in the other room.

This kid kept me hopping and utterly amazed all at once. And yet, by the time he was three years old, he still couldn't say much outside of a few words he had learned during his first year of life. I knew my boy had challenges ahead of him. Little did I know that a speech delay would be just one of many.

As I watched him turn over the letters and move them

around the table that day, trying to create his name, I reminded myself that kids learn at different ages and there was no reason to push. But I *wasn't* pushing. He wanted to spell his name, and he asked me to show him. So here we were, practicing again.

Finally, without so much as a word from me, he threw up his hands in frustration.

"It's no use!" he shouted. "My brain doesn't work right, Mom."

I was stunned. Tears welled up in my eyes. My mind swirled in confusion as he stormed off. *Why would he say that?* I wondered. I'd never said anything to make him think that.

I will never forget that moment. It was a turning point for me as a mother. That day, Cody articulated something I couldn't see and that neither of us could understand at the time.

But this statement would have tremendous ramifications for both of our lives.

The Meaning of Movement

The first thing I remember about Cody when he was born is his beauty. I couldn't stop staring at his flawless face and heavenly head of hair. I caressed his cheeks, inhaled his scent, and did everything I could not to eat him alive. After a peaceful, natural birth at the local midwifery center, I felt my oxytocin levels soaring, and my bonding with Cody was in overdrive.

The second thing I remember, but rarely thought about until much later, is that he didn't cry. I was so drawn to this mysterious little bundle, my stoic, angel-faced boy, that I failed to notice he had missed a critical marker of development.

Cody was growing just as he should. He was healthy and happy and the delight of everyone who knew him. He was checking off milestones like a champ.

Like other babies, he hated being on his tummy. But as soon as he learned how to roll onto his back, he made sure to do it immediately whenever I put him down. He learned to move by propelling himself in circles with one leg until he could scoot around the house on his back like an upside-down inchworm.

One afternoon, I found him in a bedroom on the opposite side of the house and scolded his five-year-old brother for carrying him back there without telling me.

"I didn't do it, Mom," Wyatt said. "He scooted back here on his own."

We all thought Cody's inventive, quirky mode of transportation was adorable. What we didn't realize was that it was a symptom of something more significant.

I confess that, as a new mother five times over, I wasn't always concerned with movement. My goal was to help my babies be as comfortable as possible while learning to be independent, all the while feeling as loved as possible. Most times, this meant toting my little ones around in carriers, keeping them nestled next to my body in slings, or letting them play in bouncy seats.

Whenever it was time to play, I allowed them to crawl and move however it suited them. When it didn't always look textbook, I assumed all babies had their own unique way of moving. We also used Exersaucers, bouncy seats, and Bumbo chairs.

Author and chiropractor Lindsay Mumma wrote, "Your child will learn to move on his own. And if he isn't allowed to learn on his own, he won't learn how to do it properly. That means that if you try to teach your child how to roll over, how to sit up, how to stand, how to walk, or how to run, he won't be doing it in the most efficient manner possible. Placing your child in a position that he is not able to hold himself will actually prevent him from learning how to achieve that position."[1]

Research shows us that movement is vital to brain development during the first year of life. We hear about the importance of movement, but I don't think we hear enough about *why* it is important.

If our babies roll over, crawl, and walk, does it really matter how they do it? Many doctors and researchers say that it does.

In the mid-twentieth century, Glenn Doman and his team of researchers studied the movement of babies all over the world—from the time they were in the womb to the time they were walking. Doman worked with renowned brain surgeon Temple Fay to understand how babies' brains developed and what human functions resulted. They discovered that no matter their cultural background, all babies undergo the same developmental sequence of mobility.

This developmental sequence begins in utero and continues until around six years of age for girls and eight years of age for boys, with an additional boost in adolescence. It is composed of mobility, sensory, and reflex stimulation and moves up through the brain—pons level, midbrain, and cortex.

Biologically, all children must go through this sequence of developmental movement to obtain optimal brain function. With proper and positive stimulation, this sequence occurs naturally, growing and building a child's brain, synapse upon synapse. When there are negative factors in a developing child's environment, it can cause certain genes to turn off, disrupting the developmental sequence.

Brain science shows that a disrupted mobility sequence can manifest in a number of ways: sensory disorders, self-regulation issues, language or learning challenges. It can show up as autism, Asperger's, ADHD, or oppositional disorders. It can look sullen and moody or wild and disruptive, depending on which side of the brain missed a step, so to speak, in development.[2]

These missteps in sequence can occur for any number of reasons. It sounds dramatic to call it trauma, but all of us experience trauma to varying degrees, sometimes even unidentifiable ones.

There is obvious trauma, of course, like physical or emotional abuse. But there are other kinds of traumatic experiences that children can undergo. Birth trauma, a minor brain injury like a concussion, or a major illness are different types of trauma that could potentially lead to a developmental gap. Even anesthesia in children under two can have an effect on the neuroreceptors that need to develop.

Unintentional trauma could also be the result of stress (maternal or childhood), environmental toxins (like pesticides or poisons), overexposure to radiation (multiple ultrasounds or too much screen time), poor nutrition, or undiagnosed allergies or food sensitivities.

While trauma can be something bad that happens, it can also be something good that *doesn't* happen in a child's life, like not having a loving parent, a connection with a committed caregiver, tender physical touch, good nutrition, a safe emotional environment, or a healthy physical movement.

Research shows that the two most important factors for a developing child are movement and a parent's touch.[3]

The good news is that even if the steps in this developmental sequence get bypassed in the first year or two of life, brain researchers have discovered that by re-creating the developmental sequence of mobility, we can help the brain regain the functions to self-correct these missteps.

Doman's findings and work have been used to rehabilitate stroke victims, the mentally impaired, and people with brain traumas. The key isn't unlocking a cure for the symptoms, but the cause.

This issue certainly isn't addressed in the average baby book. Trust me, as an avid researcher, I've read lots of them. There's a plethora of positive offerings to help parents get through those tough early years, but nothing about movement and neurology.

I still remember a conversation with my son's pediatrician at his three-month wellness checkup:

"How much tummy time is he getting each day?" the pediatrician asked.

"Oh, I don't know," I said, thinking back to the parenting books I had read during pregnancy. "Maybe ten to fifteen minutes." I paused. "But he seems to hate being on his tummy. Is that normal?"

"Well, most babies do," she said laughing. "Just keep doing the best you can."

That was it. End of story. I felt slightly relieved. *It must not be all that important*, I thought to myself.

I only wish I had known at the time just how important movement is. How tummy time leads to tummy crawling, a necessary piece of the sequence. How tummy crawling leads to hands-and-knees creeping, the more obvious "crawl." How tummy crawling and hands-and-knees creeping each have their place before walking. How my baby's mobility sequence was as important as the nourishment and nurturing I gave him.

Fast-forward to the day I was standing behind Cody at the table. It had been almost seven years of watching him thrive in so many ways but struggle in others. Three years of working on his letters to no avail. Two years of watching him "write" in his morning journal "symbols" he could not decipher. And yet another year of watching him write his name: Y D O C.

The day my son told me his brain didn't work right—that

was the day that changed the course of our lives. That was the day I committed to learning *how* his beautiful brain worked.

The Telltale Signs

Cody was the child who helped himself. He waited for no one to do what he was confident he could do. He was a tinkerer, a figure-it-outer, a risk-taker, and a decision-maker. As a result, he had his first set of stitches before he was two years old and had to get staples in his head twice before he was three. He didn't cry through any of it. It was as if he felt no pain. As it turns out, he didn't feel any (or hardly any).

Doctors were amazed by his bravery and his strength of spirit. I admit that I was too. At least for a while. Aside from a speech delay and his subsequent dyslexia and learning challenges, Cody developed normally. No aberrant behavior, no unusual quirks like tics or obsessions. In fact, he was an easy child.

Until he wasn't.

At seven years old, with seemingly no cause for it, he began demonstrating fight-or-flight tendencies, often even resisting our love and protection. And most disturbing, he began hitting himself on the head when he became frustrated.

What we chalked up to being passionate and perfection-driven was really an expression of one side of his brain in overdrive, overcompensating for gaps in the other side. At some point in his growth and development (we won't ever fully know), his brain got a little out of balance.

His early learning challenges led to behavioral challenges, which led to emotional challenges, which left us all feeling helpless. You see, when you're living in a state of fight or flight, you cannot feel safe. If you don't feel safe, you don't feel loved. And if you don't feel loved, it's nearly impossible to behave in an emotionally healthy way. That's no way to learn. And that's no way to live.

I have a remarkable son. If this were his brag book, we'd be here for days. But the challenges of an apparent learning disorder and the continual stress on his central nervous system turned our lives into a constant balancing act. There were days (and sometimes weeks) at a time when interacting was a struggle on both of our parts. He was trying to make sense of the confusion, frustration, and subsequent anger that were the result of having an overactive amygdala. And we were trying not to set off any land mines on the battle-worn terrain of his heart.

We looked into various approaches for helping Cody with his learning disabilities. But most of them just didn't sit right. We didn't want a coping mechanism for a perceived problem but rather a key to unlocking the potential of who he was made to be. We knew from our research into the science of how the brain works that if neuroplasticity was our brain's natural superpower, then there had to be a way to repattern the brain for optimal learning and living.

Through a ton of research and a whole lot of faith, we came to the belief that if a brain could become disorganized, then it could become organized again.

We were determined to help our child not merely survive but also thrive.

Shifting Our Perspective

The brain is the most complex organ in the human body with over eighty-six billion neurons, or nerve cells, that communicate with other neurons, creating trillions of connections and making countless circuits to form the body's nervous system. It's an incredible system, but also very fragile. With so many pathways, there are countless ways for things to go in a different direction.

Disruptions in our neurology may act as minor traumas to the brain. We often think of trauma as major, life-altering events. But trauma isn't caused only by a physical or emotional incident. Injuries to the brain can also occur without our knowing it. A high fever, a head injury, environmental toxins, stress in utero, and limited motor activities in the first two years of life are just a few of the ways that a brain can become disorganized.[4]

There is still so much we don't know about the brain, but many scientists, doctors, and psychiatrists have devoted their lives to unraveling the mysteries of the mind, and we're learning more every day.

Less than a hundred years ago, it was widely accepted that the brain was rigid. However, today, we know that the brain is actually extremely malleable. Experts call this "plasticity."

Just as we are able to create new neuropathways with new information, physical activity, and external experiences, we can create new circuits and pathways in the areas that are out of balance, essentially rewiring our brains. This monumental discovery has changed the field of brain research, not to mention the practical application of such a profound understanding.

I think it's one of the most important discoveries for parents today. Most parenting philosophies don't account for the complexity of our children's neurology. But the brain affects everything from how we feel and express our emotions to how we behave and respond in certain situations. While the brain might be stuck in certain patterns, it doesn't have to remain stuck.

Doctors Daniel J. Siegel and Tina Payne Bryson wrote a revolutionary book for parents called *The Whole-Brain Child*.

They took their research on the brain and applied it to children, showing how parents can help their children navigate their thoughts and emotions, no matter how big or small. Their goal was to explain how the brain works and help us nurture our children in the way they need to grow into healthy, happy, and resilient adults.

They wrote, "We aren't held captive for the rest of our lives by the way the brain works at this moment—we can actually rewire it so that we can be healthier and happier. This is true not only for children and adolescents, but also for each of us across the life span."[5]

What this means is that while we may be born with a neurological imbalance or suffer a brain injury in our lifetime, there is hope for restoring neurological function. What has been lost can also be restored. What may present itself as a disability can be turned into a superpower.

Many people still believe that most of our children's "challenges" are the result of poor parenting. I'm not dismissing the role of the parent, not by any means. I believe in the power of parenting, the crucial connections that only we can provide, and the sacred responsibility each of us has to raise up these precious souls in a loving home. But what if our children's behavior wasn't solely a result of irresponsible parenting? What if it was a result of neurology?

How would that change our perspective on our children and transform our relationships? Perhaps it would turn our parenting paradigm on its head.

Fighting for Our Children

I was sitting in a hotel room in Greenville, South Carolina, when I got a text from my friend Paula: "I'm at an informational meeting all about the brain, and I keep thinking about you. You need to look up NeuroDevelopmental Movement when you get a chance."

I spent the rest of the night poring over the organization's website.

Through this organization, I got connected with Addilynn Holloman, who is a mother of three boys. With a background in education, she has always had a desire to help children learn. But when her eldest son was five years old, Addilynn was repeatedly confronted with the reality that she couldn't teach her own child. He wasn't responsive to normal educational experiences, even natural learning opportunities. He rarely engaged, was often in his own world, and would even walk past her without noticing.

"I couldn't get through to him," she recalled. "I couldn't get into his world."

While she knew there was plenty of "help" for the symptoms he was demonstrating, she wanted to uncover *why* he was having them. In true mama fashion, she spent hours googling learning techniques, developmental therapies, and brain research. She found a video by neurological therapist Nina Jonia, talking about the developmental sequence that occurs in children and what happens when it is disrupted. After watching only half of the video, Addilynn closed her laptop and wept.

"She was describing my reality," Addilynn said. "She was describing my oldest—and subsequently my two youngest, as well."

The next day, she set up an appointment with Nina at NeuroDevelopmental Movement and flew to Oregon to meet with her. The founders of this program have mostly passed on, but others, like Nina, have taken up the torch to continue educating, training, and working with clients.

Three months after using the program, Addilynn started seeing changes in her son's personality. He learned how to ride a bike and swim underwater, two things he wasn't able to do because of his lack of spatial awareness. He began to engage willingly, and his attention span grew by leaps and bounds.

Most parents think all their children's issues are behavior related. That we can parent the problems right out of them. That we can teach them to show empathy or not to throw fits. That we can help them learn to read with the proper instruction. But the aha moment came to Addilynn when she realized it wasn't the behavior she needed to fix, but the gap in neurological function.

After seeing such significant results in such a short time, Addilynn knew she couldn't keep this to herself. Her desire to help other children learn and grow never left, and she decided to go through the training to become a developmental movement consultant, in order to help other families.

For the past two years, Addilynn has been working with our family to help Cody reach his fullest potential. Each and every day, we repeat movements that can help restore what has been undone.

"Movement creates sensory experiences and reflex integration that in turn trigger the brain's growth and ability to process and interpret the perceived information," Addilynn said. "This work erases the myth of impossibility because it is a plan not made by man, but is a plan set forth from the beginning of time to help the brain grow from the bottom up, just as a child develops naturally."

Make no mistake, the neurological movement program has nothing to do with "fixing" children. There is absolutely nothing wrong with their beautiful minds. On the contrary, this love work is about removing the barriers that keep them from fully expressing themselves—mind, body, and heart.

About a year after starting the program, Cody stopped hitting himself in the head and destroying things. Now, after two years of moving through the developmental sequence, he is not only reading sequentially but progressing daily at a rapid speed. And, of course, he's continuing to fix home appliances when they break, engineering actual working canons out of cardboard, and brainstorming ways to rid the world of plastic and save the oceans and their inhabitants.

Letters no longer look like symbols to decipher but sounds to discover—and, most importantly, remember. He can self-regulate and recover from disappointment. He loses his temper like the rest of us but recognizes the consequences of his actions. He can feel pain and hunger and is learning how to regulate these newfound feelings.

He's still the same sweet, smart boy, only we get to see more of him. He's still a rash responder. He just recovers quicker. He's still a brilliant inventor. He just thinks and expresses himself more clearly.

We aren't quite finished with the program yet, but we're nearing the end. The time of recreating the developmental sequences to make connections in the brain will be over soon, but the outcomes will last his lifetime. What I'm most grateful for isn't that he's less of himself, but more.

Unbridling the Brilliance

I know what some of you might be thinking: *My dyslexic child is brilliant. I don't want to "cure" them of anything.* And I agree 100 percent. My husband and I had the same conversation early on. We didn't want Cody to be different. We didn't want to change the beauty of his brilliance. His neurodivergence makes him better, not worse. It is not only an integral part of who he is. It's also a blessing.

The outcome is not changing who he is but rather optimizing his unique gifts.

It's removing the roadblocks that keep him from the whole of his potential.

Helping our children's brains function more effectively doesn't change their intellectual genius. It only enhances it. It helps them think clearer, process information faster, and engage more effectively. It helps them become whole.

Just imagine your brilliant little boy or girl not having to work so hard simply to process information. All that effort could be directed toward learning, ideating, doing, and creating.

Most parents I talk to admit they're in a state of survival. There are many days when I feel the same way. While survival might seem like the best outcome in some seasons, most of us desire for more than just survival. We want to thrive. And more than anything, we want our kids to thrive.

Parenting often feels like battle. Making meals, getting everyone dressed, supervising schoolwork, getting them to sports practice, co-op, and piano lessons. Not to mention the bickering, back talk, disrespect, and sibling rivalry. Some days, we're not sure we can keep doing it. I get it.

Sometimes we forget what we're fighting for, and we end up directing our frustration toward our kids. But the battle isn't *with* them, it's *for* them.

There are times when we know something isn't quite right with our children. Their pediatrician may not be concerned, their teachers may not be worried, and our children seem to be "on track." But as parents, we are our children's best advocates. We have to dig deep at times, observe them closely, conduct the research, and do what it takes to find answers to help them.

Friend, can I say something? As parents, we can beat ourselves up for the struggles our children may have. We feel the weight of responsibility. But if you're in this situation, it isn't your fault. I promise. You are doing an amazing job. Feel free to grieve, and then move on.

Whatever you do, don't blame yourself, your spouse, or any other person who comes to mind. It's important not to dwell on the *how*, but rather the *help*. The goal of neurodevelopment is not to fix something that is broken, because it isn't. Your child is not broken.

The goal is to unlock greater potential. It is only once we can love and accept our children the way they are, celebrating every aspect of them, that we can begin to dream and envision their future.

If my job as a parent is to equip my child for life, then I want to do everything I can to help restore what's been lost. If there are certain brain functions that will help them have the kind of quality of life that I envision for them, I am going to do whatever I can to help them.

I always knew that I would share the story of our family, of our struggles and our triumphs. I just didn't know it would come so soon. But there are moments when you know it's time to pass on what you know, even if it isn't much. Through it all, I want to offer hope.

Hope that you aren't alone.

Hope that there are answers.

Hope that you can do this.

11

TO PURSUE
A VISION

All we have to decide is what to do
with the time that is given us.

—GANDALF THE GREY IN *THE FELLOWSHIP*
OF THE RING BY J. R. R. TOLKIEN

I n the spring of 2018, we were getting ready to take
possession of a fifty-acre tract of raw land near the Blue
Ridge Mountains of Virginia for what was supposed to
become the Wild + Free Farm Village. It was a dream that
Ben, I, and others in the Wild + Free community had had for a
while—a place for families to connect with each other, make
memories together, and let their children run wild and free.

The Wild + Free community had come together to raise
$392,000 for a place where we could host mama retreats,
getaways for teens, and weekend experiences for families. The
place we found wasn't big, but it had a dramatic terrain, rushing
streams, and gorgeous mountain views.

We had a ratified contract in hand but had asked for a contingency period so we could do our due diligence. We needed to check for water underground, analyze soil types for

drain fields, and get clearance from the zoning board for our intended use of the land.

Everything checked out. There was ample water. The septic engineer assured us that he could devise a solution for a large event barn. And we identified several areas of the parcel that would be perfect for lodging.

Even the zoning commissioner was agreeable. But she recommended that we meet with the neighbors to share our plans before the issue came to a vote at the next planning meeting.

"You don't want any surprises," she told us.

Our real estate agent set up a meeting at a little country church where many of the neighbors were members. We traveled there on the appointed weekend to attend a service in the morning and prepare for the meeting later that night. We were able to introduce our family and meet some of the nicest people you could ever hope to meet. After such a warm experience that morning, we assumed the town hall meeting was going to be a breeze. In fact, we wondered if anyone would waste a perfectly good Sunday evening and bother to show up at all.

We could not have been more wrong.

That evening, the parking lot was so packed with cars that we could hardly find a spot for our own. We tried greeting folks as we walked in, but something was clearly afoul. They would hardly even look at us. They might as well have been carrying pitchforks and torches.

We took our seat at the table in front of the room and braced ourselves for the onslaught.

These people clearly didn't want us there. Most of them sat there glaring at us, arms folded across their chests. A few of them stood up and lectured us, pointing their fingers at us, their bodies shaking with disdain. They took turns describing all the ways we were about to destroy their lives.

They complained about the traffic we would bring. The loss of the land, which had been owned by the same family for generations. The life-threatening risk of having a zip line (which we had mentioned on our website). And one man even warned us that our children had better wear orange vests during hunting season or who knows what might happen. I couldn't help but ask the man if he was threatening our kids. He happened to be the deputy sheriff of the county. I felt like we were in a Stephen King novel.

To make matters worse, our children observed all this with us. It wasn't exactly the joyous learning experience we had hoped it would be.

In the middle of that meeting, Ben and I turned and looked at each other. We knew it was over. We surrendered the property and walked away from the contract.

Dream Big Dreams

We returned home without a backup plan and with no clue what to do next. We explained to our kids that it wasn't meant to be, but deep down, we couldn't understand why.

Friends implored us to find land in Missouri or West Virginia. And apparently there is some highly affordable real estate in parts of Kentucky. But unless we wanted the property to sit idle most of the time, we needed to be close enough to host gatherings there.

What's more, purchasing a large parcel of land for $392,000 isn't easy unless you're okay with long, drooping power lines that cut across the property or strange easements that allow strangers to do whatever they'd like on your land at any given time.

We stopped searching for several months, but the dream never died. The calling became louder and stronger, but without a clear path forward, we could only watch and wait.

Finally, one Saturday morning in the summer of 2018, Ben and I were sitting in bed, drinking coffee, when I decided to pull out my phone and scan Zillow. I opened the app, refreshed the listings with a quick swipe of my thumb, and a new listing appeared for a property in Head Waters, Virginia.

It was a fully developed retreat center on 197 acres, complete with a lodge that housed fifty-two beds, a dining hall, and a commercial kitchen. It also had a ropes course, a zip line, several staff houses, cabins, a bed-and-breakfast, and access to thousands of acres in the adjoining national forest.

The asking price was $3.2 million.

I showed the listing to Ben, and he dismissed it immediately: it was far too expensive. But something made us take a second look. The property took our breath away. We could envision the Wild + Free community coming to a place like this. It would accelerate our vision by at least twenty years. We looked at each other.

"Why not?" I asked. "It doesn't hurt to check it out."

Ben called the real estate agent and learned that she had just posted the listing that morning, the very minute I had discovered it.

"Come out this Wednesday," she said.

So we did. We walked the trails, visited the cabins, and dreamed inside the lodge. We never told her that we couldn't afford the place. She wouldn't have wasted another second on us if we had. We told her that we would think about it and get back to her. We made the long trip back home in silence.

The next day, I was scrolling through photos I had taken of the property, and there was the beautiful old farmhouse from the mid-nineteenth century that had been remodeled as a bed-and-breakfast. It looked familiar, but I couldn't place it right away. I opened Instagram, wondering if I had seen it there when I suddenly remembered a post by my friend Bethany. She and her husband Garrett had traveled through Virginia with their family several months prior and had stayed at the property. And there it was on her feed.

We called our friends and learned that not only had they stayed there but they were also good friends with the president of the organization that owned the property. They had run it as a youth camp for the past thirty years, but they felt it was time to sell. Bethany and Garrett offered to reach out to the president on our behalf and make an introduction.

It felt like a long shot, but if we've learned anything, it's to never say no for other people. Our job is to dream big and make big asks. It's other people's job to say yes or no.

We had many conversations with the president over the next year. He even came to Virginia Beach to have dinner with us and learn more about our vision. No matter how much he came down in price—$2 million, $1.4 million, and finally $1 million—we couldn't budge from the $392,000 we had raised.

Other parties were interested in buying the place, but for some reason the president never said no to us. And as long as that word never came out of his mouth, we believed it was possible.

Not long after, Ben and I were at the Wild + Free Conference in Frisco, Texas, stuffing attendee bags in the back of the arena with our team when Ben got the text message that changed our lives:

"Okay, we'll do it for $425,000."

We took possession of the property in August 2019 and have since overhauled the lodge with fresh paint and new carpet. We've refurbished the old farmhouse and replaced the zip lines. We've installed new bathhouses for camping and fixed up the staff house, among other things.

We've hosted a number of retreats, camping weekends, and festivals and look forward to hosting many more. In fact, we have a dream of starting Wild + Free farm villages all over the country. This is just the beginning of an exciting future for this community.

The Farm Village is not just a miraculous turn of events for the Wild + Free community. It's also a testament to the power of dreaming big. And our family, along with the dozens of families that have gathered around us to give, serve, work, and help, has forever been changed by this story. My kids can dream bigger, aim higher, and attempt great things because they know that all things are possible.

Let us not merely live together as a family going through the motions of day-to-day life. Let's dream of what's possible when we're unafraid to band together and do hard things.

Your Great Gift to the World

Your family didn't end up together by accident. The unique personalities, skills, and temperaments in your home were placed there for a distinct purpose. Your family was brought together for such a time as this, to accomplish something that only you could do together.

Your family has a great gift to offer the world.

Maybe it's to raise up a family of artists or musicians, like our friends Clint and Sandy Hunt, who homeschooled all seven of their children and taught them how to sing and play instruments. Their band, the Hunts, grew up touring the country and have performed at many of our Wild + Free conferences. Clint and Sandy both play instruments and have a special knack for teaching kids. It was meant to be.

Maybe your family's purpose is to inspire other families with your perseverance through difficult times or how you care for each other's learning challenges or physical disabilities. It could be your story of overcoming marital challenges and emboldening other couples to not give up.

Or maybe your family's purpose is to raise up a particular child who has a unique calling in life. Consider Alberta Williams King, Martin Luther King Jr.'s mother, who taught him that segregation was a "social condition rather than a natural order."[1] Or Nancy Edison, mother of Thomas Edison, who homeschooled him when his teachers called him "addled" and to whom he attributed his success.[2] Or Abigail May Alcott, mother of Louisa May Alcott, the inspiration for Marmee in *Little Women*. Alcott claimed, "Marmee, good though she was, was still not half good enough to do justice to the real woman who inspired her."[3]

Our friends Dan and Rachel Kovac have blessed people and organizations all over the world through their generosity. They've mastered the art of having hot meals delivered to friends' houses, volunteering to help those in need, and supporting causes that are important to them. This isn't just their nature. It's their family's great gift to the world.

When the oldest of their six children, Jude, was a baby, Dan worked for an easygoing company with flexible work hours.

After watching their neighbor pull in the driveway late every night after working long days away from his three children, the Kovacs vowed, "That will never be us!"

They saw themselves as a nontraditional family and dreamed of becoming entrepreneurs together and sharing the responsibilities of both childcare and work. They spent many snowy Wisconsin mornings talking over steaming cups of coffee about how they might make their dreams a reality.

Then one frosty December afternoon, Dan got a phone call about a job opportunity in Texas. The pay was significantly higher, but so was the workload and the hours.

"We thought we would try it, just for a few years," Rachel said. "It would give Dan more experience. We could save up some money. It would never be permanent, though. That lifestyle was just not for us."

That was fifteen years ago. The Kovacs are still living in Texas, and Dan is still working for the same company.

During those first five years, Dan and Rachel experienced a lot of restlessness and angst as they tried to grasp their family's purpose. They knew they had only one chance at parenting and living their life together, and they didn't want to waste it.

Initially, Dan tried to get his old job back, but the company was shrinking, and his former colleagues were losing their jobs. On top of this, the Kovac family was growing, and Dan worried about losing their stability. They considered jobs in other parts of the country, but none of the opportunities felt right.

After their second child was born, Dan and Rachel decided to adopt their third child from Ethiopia. Dan had grown up in the jungles of Liberia before he went away to boarding school in Côte d'Ivoire, and this background gave the Kovacs a renewed passion for Africa.

"After we adopted our daughter and spent time in Ethiopia,

we felt compelled to sell everything we had and move there," Rachel said. "We would start a nonprofit. We would make a difference!"

But as the Kovacs spoke with various nonprofit directors, they were told the same thing by all of them. They didn't need more Americans moving abroad. What they lacked were the resources to make their visions achievable and their work sustainable.

"This made so much sense to us," Rachel said. "Dan's experience had shown him how important it is to pour into local economies. We had an epiphany: What if our role in making the difference we so longed to make was as ordinary and unromantic as him continuing to work in his current role so we could support organizations that are making an enormous difference in the world?"

Their journey toward contentment was a process of learning to see and experience the good they had been given, instead of clinging to a vision for something else they thought they needed. Dan still works long hours, and sometimes that isn't easy for their family. But they have found ways to prioritize connection, both with their own family and others.

"Our family mission is to love one another deeply and to love those who are brought into our path," Rachel said. "We are exactly where we were always meant to be, even when we couldn't see it."

Your Family's Vision

We often overlook our powerful purpose. We spend a lifetime chasing sales goals, pursuing recognition or positions of power in our industry, or building homes that will eventually no longer suit our lifestyles—when our greatest accomplishment could very well be sleeping in a crib or a bunk bed down the hall.

The clues to your family vision are found in the skills that you, your spouse, and your kids possess. The experiences you've had. Where you live. The opportunities in front of you. And, quite frankly, the trial and error of doing things that reveal what you prefer, what's possible, and what bears fruit.

If you notice certain injustices in the world, it means you have the eyes to see them. You've been given a mandate to use your gifts and talents to do something about them by the mere fact that you care so deeply. Otherwise, you would have hardly noticed them at all.

To discern your purpose, host a family meeting. Talk about it together. Share your dreams and desires. Do all that is in your heart. Some things will work out, and others won't. And that's okay. What some people call failure is actually a productive step toward finding your family's purpose.

Sometimes that means checking off things you don't like. Full-time RVing isn't for everybody. Owning livestock can break your heart.

Some things look impossible, and they're meant to appear that way. It's what keeps your vision from being copied or commandeered by just anyone else. If anyone could do it, then it wouldn't be your unique calling. The difficulty of your dream is what keeps the riffraff out.

Oh, and just for the record, some things aren't as impossible as they seem. Stepping forward as far as you can go will activate a series of events you could never have predicted.

There's a way. There's always a way.

And make no mistake, vision cannot be borrowed or franchised like a fast-food restaurant. You won't find it by trying to replicate the life of someone else, just like they can't be fulfilled by replicating yours. Your great gift to the world is meant for you—and you alone.

When all else fails, pay attention to what you complain about. Identify a great need or some outstanding problem in the world that your family cares about and go after it. We need your family to do what you were put here on this Earth to do. We need you to go after your family vision.

Your family was made for this moment.

12

TO BECOME TOGETHER

There is no place so awake and alive
as the edge of becoming.

—SUE MONK KIDD

O ne of my most cherished books from childhood,
The Velveteen Rabbit by Margery Williams, tells
the story of a stuffed rabbit who becomes real
through the love of a little boy. At the beginning
of his journey, he meets the wise Skin Horse, who explains
what becoming real actually means:

> *"Real isn't how you are made," said the Skin Horse. "It's a*
> *thing that happens to you. When a child loves you for a long,*
> *long time, not just to play with, but REALLY loves you, then*
> *you become Real."*
> *"Does it hurt?" asked the Rabbit.*
> *"Sometimes," said the Skin Horse, for he was always*
> *truthful. "When you are Real you don't mind being hurt."*

"Does it happen all at once, like being wound up," he asked, "or bit by bit?"

"It doesn't happen all at once," said the Skin Horse. "You become. It takes a long time. That's why it doesn't often happen to people who break easily, or have sharp edges, or who have to be carefully kept. Generally, by the time you are Real, most of your hair has been loved off, and your eyes drop out and you get loose in the joints and very shabby. But these things don't matter at all, because once you are Real you can't be ugly, except to people who don't understand."

Oh, friend, who you were meant to be isn't how you were originally made. It's a thing that happens to you after a long, long time of loving others and being loved by them, after childhood and teenage years and finally leaving home and having a family of your own.

And once you have a family, it's becoming together with them. And perhaps you never arrive, but you continue becoming through all the celebrations and challenges of life until each of you is shaped into the person you were meant to be. And none of this could have happened without the others.

How I wish becoming wasn't so hard.

I can relate to the feeling of having my hair rubbed off, having my eyes drop out, and losing my buttons. Sometimes I look in the mirror and see the joy and experience and, yes, also the heaviness that has come from years of living life: the betrayal and the rejection but also the love and the delight. I'm like that old Skin Horse who might have been ugly, but only to those who don't understand.

Let me tell you how well I've been loved. So well loved. I would never trade any of those bumps and bruises for who I am and who I have become.

And I have a family that has joined me on this journey. My husband is becoming. My children are becoming. I am becoming. And we are all becoming together.

Becoming doesn't take place overnight. It happens over seasons of hard-fought battles and through dark nights. It continues over a lifetime and includes a million mishaps and small but mighty miracles.

For every page of a storybook written are a dozen crumpled papers on the floor.

This is an important principle for every new parent to understand. We consummate love and produce children, and when they come out of the womb, we haven't any clue who they will be. We know who we *want* them to be. But they very often don't live up to our expectations.

Of course they don't. They haven't become yet.

The children we wish were studious or organized are neither, and after longing to raise a basketball team, none of the children are athletic, preferring instead to construct model airplanes and know their dates and histories. The children we wish would pay attention or stand at attention or not throw a tantrum in Target check none of those boxes, so we whisk them away to the car where we scold them for not knowing any better. But of course they don't know any better. They haven't become yet.

I know. I've given all the excuses when one of my children has made a public spectacle out of me.

"She's tired."

"She's having an off day."

"I don't know what's wrong with her."

But it's never the whole truth. She does this frequently and often at the most inopportune times.

We walk around like Jeremy Renner in *The Hurt Locker*

trying not to set off a bomb while simultaneously trying to deactivate it. We try to hide our children's becoming from the rest of the world.

The relationships we have with the people in our families are a work in progress. But we shouldn't have to hide them. All of us are on this journey of becoming together.

I often feel like there should be yellow tape cordoning off our house with a sign that says, "Under construction." The truth is, there isn't a family that exists without problems. And yet we all think we're the only ones.

So we lock our doors, shut our blinds, and ignore the doorbell for fear of what people might think if they only knew—saw—what a mess we were. Unkempt hair and sassy attitudes. The smell of burnt eggs from breakfast and a mound of laundry on the living room sofa begging to be folded.

We welcome people into our lives when our faces are fresh, our house is tidy, and our kids are uncommonly calm. I get it. There's nothing wrong with putting your best foot forward. But I've decided that for me and my family, we won't hide who and what we are—a family becoming together.

We Too Are Becoming

We become parents the moment our children are conceived, but that doesn't mean we know how to do this. We make mistakes as we go, hoping we can reconcile our shortcomings before our children grow up, before they leave the house and remain scarred for life. We count on it, in fact.

There are sins of *commission*, and there are sins of *omission*: the things we've done and, sometimes worse, the things we *haven't* done. And children can spend the rest of their lives trying to recover from either what they received and shouldn't have or what they didn't receive but desperately needed.

Our firstborns are the test cases. We don't know what we're doing, so we try everything on them. Safeguarding their every move. Sleep training. Letting them cry through naps. Dressing them in all the cute clothes. Enrolling them in programs. Controlling what they watch and what goes into their mouths.

And then the next child comes along, and everything goes out the window. The third child hardly has any restrictions at all. And heaven help the fifth child in our family, who is basically a six-year-old hippie.

We often joke about how the baby of the family grows up under completely different circumstances than the first one, but it's true. We parent our follow-up children differently because we learn that all our overprotection wasn't necessary, and their character doesn't rise and fall on one action alone.

As parents of children who are becoming, we eventually see that the process of raising them is more important than the final product. Focusing on the process over a product means you never stop seeing the potential, but you refuse to give power to mere performance. As novelist Willa Cather said, quoting the French historian Jules Michelet: "The end is nothing, the road is all."[1]

There's a reason why grandparents often make better parents to our children than they were to us. They needed our entire childhoods to become who they were meant to be. To round off those sharp edges. To gain distance from their own childhood trauma. To see the importance of connection.

Sitting in my counselor's office, I watch her lean forward and look deep into my eyes. I've just told her about a particular hurt that was caused by someone who experienced an even deeper hurt in their own past.

"Maybe their restraint was their gift to you," she says. "They couldn't stop themselves from hurting you, but it wasn't as severe as what they experienced. They could at least offer you that."

I had never seen it that way before. That they could have passed along the same hurt if they wanted to, but they held back. Yes, they hurt me, but it wasn't as severe as what they had experienced.

Our families were put together for a purpose. We were made to become who we are meant to be, not by accident, but by sharing life together in one household. While each of us is busy growing as an individual, our families are also growing together. We rub against each other, rub one another the wrong way, and rub off the good and bad characteristics, just as iron sharpens iron.

It can be hard. And it can splinter families that aren't prepared for just how difficult it is. But if we keep going, if we refuse to throw in the towel and succumb to our blaring inadequacies, we'll eventually be transformed into the people we never could have become apart.

This is the act of becoming.

Recovering from Past Hurts

Recovering from hurts can be just as painful of a process as experiencing them. But until we recover, we can't heal. If we can't heal, we get stuck. And when we get stuck, we stop becoming.

My daughter recently had a few rough days of playing with her brothers. She's seven years old and has a tender heart and a fierce will. She's determined to show her brothers she can be "one of the guys," with their rough handling and joke-telling.

But last week, she was weary. I could see it. I encouraged her to play apart from them for a while, but it was too late. One too many hurts had made her faint of heart.

That evening, we were getting ready for a family bike ride, and she had a complete meltdown. It was quite out of character for her, and her response was disproportionate for the situation. But there she was, sobbing on the side of the road in front of our house, her pain worsened by a rock inside her shoe.

The adult in me wanted to tell her to pull herself together. It wasn't that bad. We needed to keep moving to catch up. But the mother in me pulled her close. I told her it was okay to cry, that I knew she had had a hard couple of days. I told her she just needed to let it out and I would hold her.

I've realized that when my child's emotions are bigger than the situation warrants, they have pent-up hurt they need to release. I wanted to give her the time and space to do that.

So I asked if she wanted to stay home, but she shook her head. She wanted to go. She rode like the wind that night. She pedaled her little heart out with renewed strength. She needed a release. Not from the tiny pebble inside her shoe but from the heap of hurt she had been holding inside for days.

Tears filled my eyes as I watched her ride. I whispered a thank-you for the momentary grace to see what she had needed, and I grieved for what I might have done in the name of rationality. I shuddered to think of all the times I hadn't seen what my kids needed and responded with logic instead of love.

A wild and free family isn't seeking perfection. As parents, we want to be the best possible parents for our children, but we also know that we're going to fail, mess up, and even screw up royally on occasion.

And we aren't just going to let our kids down. We're going to let ourselves down, as well.

For parents, it can be difficult for us to hear how we've hurt our children, especially in their own words. Sometimes their words seem harsh, hurtful, perhaps not aligned with reality. But it's important that we hear their pain when they are willing (and most importantly, needing) to express it.

That doesn't mean we shouldn't help our children develop healthy habits or invest in their character development. But we can't fix a festering wound by covering it with a Band-Aid. An infection has to be addressed before the body can heal.

As Pam Leo wrote, "Until the hurt comes out, the love can't get in."[2]

I have a friend who was raised by nannies, from her birth all the way through high school. Her own mother was present but distant. As an adult, my friend realized that having a nanny wasn't about her mother not loving her, but about her mother loving her enough to protect her, from herself.

You see, her mother grew up in orphanages, never knew her mother, and didn't trust herself to know *how* to mother. My friend's nannies were a flawed answer to a tragic problem, but they were an offering of love, not the lack thereof.

Understanding the reason for someone's failures doesn't make the impact of loss any less. But it does allow us to heal in time, move on, and do things differently going forward.

Some of us have unfathomable trauma that can't be righted simply with time and space. Some of us need therapy; others simply need someone to show us a different way, to change ineffective patterns and begin anew. But all of us need a chance to love and be loved in return.

If we want to truly love, nurture, and support our children in the ways they need, we must discard the things that prevent us from having connection, empathy, and compassion for our children.

Our children's behavioral issues are not a character problem.

Our children's behavioral issues are not a parenting problem.

Our children's behavioral issues are a symptom of something deeper: an unmet need perhaps, a depleted love tank, or an unprocessed emotion.

Commit to uncover it with gentleness.

Surrender your will to the sacred space of their safety.

Be there for their becoming.

Keep Going—It's Worth It

A few years ago, we decided to pull a ruse on the attendees of the Wild + Free conference in Portland, Oregon. A few months earlier, I had seen a video posted on Facebook of a home-schooled teenager named Leila singing and playing the ukulele. It was mesmerizing, to say the least. Leila had written a song with a beautiful melody, and her voice was so distinctive and pure that I had to hear it in person.

I reached out to her mother, Amy Hughes, and asked if I could fly them both to the conference held at the Portland Art Museum to delight the audience with a surprise performance.

I arranged for them to be called up onstage and interviewed as if they had been randomly selected from the crowd. All of it had been scripted and even rehearsed. I asked them a few questions, like whether they were enjoying the conference and how far they had come to be there.

And then, after finding out that fifteen-year-old Leila

enjoyed playing music, I invited her to "spontaneously" pick an instrument from the house band's equipment onstage and give us a demonstration. We arranged for Leila's ukulele to be strategically positioned next to the drum set where she could easily find it. When Leila walked up to the microphone and started playing, the crowd went nuts.

I apologize to the attendees of the 2018 Wild + Free Portland conference for pulling a fast one on them, but I don't apologize for what they got to experience that afternoon.

In our interview, Amy explained that Leila was a wonderful child and an even more wonderful student. She finished her work on time, read books beyond her years, and went above and beyond in all things extracurricular. Amy was positive it was due to her approach to parenting.

Until her next child came along. And the next one. And the next one. And so on. Amy joked that Leila ruined her for the other six children who followed. All her children have their own unique gifts and contributions to offer the world, and none of them are becoming like any other.

To quote Eric Clapton, Leila did nothing to ease my friend's worried mind.

While becoming is a process, it isn't another goal to achieve. It is the lack of goals, the state of being together for the long haul, that allows us to become together. In the end, while all of us will have grown and achieved individually, I will always believe we have done it together.

What I am, I am because of my children. And what they each are, they are because of each other—and hopefully a little because of their parents.

May we never judge someone else for where they might be on their journey of becoming. May we never judge ourselves for where we are. Keep going. Keep growing. Get help if you need it.

Never think you are too broken or not broken enough to seek professional care or therapy. Do whatever it takes to get back on track. To heal. To change. To become.

Love more.

Smile more.

Say yes more.

Forgive more.

Don't let a good day be ruined by a bad yesterday. New mercies rise up with each morning sun, and grace falls like rain, quenching our souls like the sun-dried earth. A hug can heal hurts, a kind word can change hearts, and laughter can soothe tension.

So much is happening under the roofs of our homes.

So much growing in both child and parent.

As Michelangelo said at the age of eighty-seven, "Ancora imparo—I am still learning."

Love Is Always Worth It

While *The Velveteen Rabbit* is a cherished book from my childhood, one of the things I remember about it as a little girl was that it often left me feeling unsettled. I think one of the reasons for this is that it exposed the truth about becoming— that to the one living outside the story, it looks *unbecoming*.

It took growing up for me to realize why.

It took getting wrinkles and crow's-feet and wily gray hairs to help me remember the wonders these eyes have witnessed and all the precious kisses that smothered my face. It took having my belly expand and retract five times over, leaving stretch marks and loose skin, for me to see my body as a marvel. It took having my breasts suckled for a total of eleven years for me to see my bosom as beautiful.

When given the choice between a skinless horse and a newly stuffed one, a child will always choose the new one. Unless *she* was the one that loved it skinless. Then nothing could ever replace it. And the skinless horse wouldn't want to be pristine if it meant being unloved.

The gray streaks in my hair and the creases around my eyes define my reflection a little more each day. But it's the stories they tell and the people who have loved them into existence that reflect the woman inside. And I grow fonder of her a little more every day.

As wrinkles settle into permanent creases and battle wounds become sacred scars, so grows the contentment in my soul. Contentment comes when we discover that we can simultaneously hold joy and sadness. It comes when we have faced so many dark nights that we find we have befriended the moon. It comes from losing our substance from constant handling but realizing that the renewing of our minds and hearts is a continual process.

I am riddled with the wear and tear of becoming.

I am shabbier and happier the more real I become.

I am the Skin Horse.

And I want to tell you that it hurts to become, but that it is worth it.

Love is always worth it.

13

TO NOT GROW WEARY

Even the darkest night will end
and the sun will rise.

—VICTOR HUGO

I have news for you, my fellow sojourner: there is no promised land of parenting. This is the heartbreaking and yet not-entirely-hopeless predicament of raising a family.

We see the promise from a distance, and it compels us to walk into parenthood with the highest ideals for what this season will offer. But then our hopes are dashed. Financial struggles, a broken marriage, the loss of a loved one, challenges with a child, and chronic illness are just a few of the things that can rattle us, if not devastate us, at one time or another.

I've experienced all of the above.

Everyone goes through hard times. And if you haven't yet, just wait. Difficulties and challenges are inevitable. The one constant in life is change. The question is not whether hard times will befall us, but what we will do when they inevitably come. Will we wander the desert, bitter and jaded, or adapt our expectations to what's best for our families and allow this new course to renew our hope?

When we follow our hearts and do what's best for our children, we will look back on our lives and realize that we had experienced a promised land after all. The only ones who miss out on it are those who fail to see the good.

I agree with the poet Atticus, who said, "The doubters are just dreamers with broken hearts."[1]

Maybe your days aren't living up to your ideals and you're already discouraged. Maybe you're wondering if you can do this after all. Just remember that your most important job is not to enforce rules, administer a schedule, or ensure that your days are filled with amazing moments. Your most important job is to know and love your children, to nurture their hearts and minds, and uncover all the hidden beauty in this season as a family.

Of course, it's not always pretty. We're broken. We have scars. We walk with a limp. But we are wounded healers and heartbroken nurturers who continue to aspire to the calling in our hearts. Do not grow weary in doing good, dear friend, for at the proper time, you will reap a harvest.

Dealing with Difficult Times

In June 2014, Wild + Free writer Renee Huston held a positive pregnancy test in her hand while she looked at her husband with a shocked grin on her face.[2] They already had three children, and this fourth pregnancy came as a surprise. She spent the rest of the summer getting through bouts of morning sickness.

By the end of August, her sickness subsided, and she began preparing for another school year. The next week, however, she felt extreme abdominal pain. Only in her second trimester, Renee went to the ER filled with trepidation.

The diagnosis? She needed an emergency appendectomy. The surgery went perfectly, her baby was unharmed, and she came home shaken but ready to recover.

Less than two weeks later, Renee's husband was putting their three kids to bed while she lay on the couch with severe back pain. Some momentary relief came, but then she was hit with crippling pain that didn't let up. She told her husband they needed to go back to the ER right away.

He called for babysitting help while Renee packed a bag and made her way down to the car. After she descended a flight of stairs, her water suddenly broke. Her crippling back pain had been back labor.

Soon after they arrived at the hospital, Renee's son was placed into her arms. "He never took a breath of stale air on Earth," Renee said, "but was safely delivered into the Lord's care."

The next week was a blur while the Huston family hastily prepared a small funeral for their son and began having difficult conversations with their other three children, ages six and under.

After the funeral ended and the out-of-town guests departed, Renee was left wondering how she could ever go on caring for her three young children, let alone homeschool them. She was still in a lot of pain from the appendectomy and was dealing with complications from her delivery.

Renee shared several ways we can make it through difficult times:

ACCEPT HELP FROM OTHERS. Renee has a self-diagnosed type-A personality and dislikes asking people for help. "But during my trial, it was necessary," she said. "I needed to embrace my community of friends who were more than willing to serve me. They dropped off dinners, canceled appointments for me, loved on my kids, included them in family outings, and made it possible for me to rest and recover. It was such a blessing to my whole family when I accepted help from our friends who loved us so much."

CHANGE YOUR PLANS. Not all seasons have to look alike. Don't be afraid to slow down, take things off your to-do list, cancel commitments, and alter your plans for a season. Because Renee homeschools her children, she was able to cancel school during this crisis. "How grateful I was that we didn't have to immediately jump into full days of lessons, school projects, and field trips," Renee said. We can incorporate this same philosophy into our family lives, whether or not we homeschool our children. This can look like taking a break from extracurricular activities when things are especially tough or accepting fewer playdate or dinner invitations when your family needs more time to unwind.

INCLUDE YOUR KIDS. Hardship provides an opportunity to draw closer to your children. "There were of course details they didn't need to know," Renee said, "but we shared our sadness and our sorrow with them. We grieved together and allowed room for spontaneous cuddling and conversations. Show them that grieving is okay, that rest and recovery is important, and that family comes first above all else."

As parents, we have passed through countless seasons, whole lifetimes, in the span of a few short years: from giving birth and raising a newborn to navigating the toddler years, helping our children grow into young, responsible humans. And in each season, we have had to learn new skills and dig deep for the fortitude and wisdom to make it through.

But parents have a magical ability to find strength in the most challenging circumstances. Sure, we get a lot wrong. But there's something inside us that presses us onward so we can do whatever it takes to help our children thrive.

Maybe this week hasn't gone as planned. Maybe you haven't found your flow yet. Maybe you're new to homeschooling, and it's proving to be even more difficult than you had imagined.

Oh, friend, you are not alone. In the midst of all the newness, excitement, and wonder, there are still the discouraging meltdowns, boycotts, and tears (and that's not even counting your kids).

When we can't control the darkness outside our doors, we can shine the light of love and hope within our homes. When we turn on the news and can't make sense of what we see, we can turn to the ones beside us and stoke the embers of connection.

In the absence of doing something great, let us do small things with great love.

In the invisible spans of heaven and earth, let us find our hope and hold tightly to that.

Perhaps we will find that love makes small things great.

Perhaps we will see that hope was there all along.

Warding Off Worry

My friend Richele Baburina once recounted the time when her eldest son, who had been homeschooled, applied for a prestigious study-abroad program.[3] He had written some wonderful essays, demonstrated his commitment to volunteering and community service, submitted his letters of recommendation, and waited with eager anticipation for the decision.

The night before Thanksgiving, he received an email that said that he was not admitted and that the selection board, which was made up of school administrators, had never accepted a homeschooler into the program.

"Fear started to hiss in my ear and say, 'I told you so,'" Richele said. "I looked at my son and said, 'I'm sorry.'

"He looked at me and said, 'Sorry for what?'

"'I'm sorry if I did you a disservice by homeschooling you,'" Richele said.

She continued, "That young man, who stands a whole head above me, looked me straight in the eye and said, 'Mom, I never want to hear you apologize to me for that again.'"

Richele said that we might not be able to look into the future lists and folders of our children, but if we could, she imagined they would look like this:

My mother listened without judgment or criticism.
She preserved my childhood.
She added kindling to my ideas and interests.
She gave me time in nature; she let me climb trees, learn at my own pace, and grapple with problems. And—most often—my mom did it with me.

Richele said, "So when fear comes whispering to you and says, 'You've got a lot to answer for. You can't possibly cover all areas in every subject with no omissions, no gaps in learning. You cannot provide your child with the most perfect toys, the most perfect environment, the most balanced diet, or nurture every good habit, allow them every opportunity to fail before they leave your house at eighteen,' give fear a nod and say, 'That's right, I can't. But you still don't get to drive.'"

There isn't a single parent of grown children who will say they didn't worry about their children, wonder if they were doing right by them, or wonder if their kids were going to turn out okay.

I worry about my children. I worry that they'll never outgrow their temper. I worry that they won't want to go to college. That they won't learn to tie their shoes. That they won't have a successful relationship. That they'll never make it in the real world.

If you're a homeschooling parent like me, these feelings may be all the more compounded by the thought that the burden of educating your children falls solely on you—or on you and your spouse.

In her twenty-third book, *Awaking Wonder*, Sally Clarkson shared the journey of raising four souls to be wonder seekers and world changers. She knew people wanted an inside peek at her practices, so she drew them into her story and divulged her secret parenting hack.

It wasn't curriculum. In fact, she didn't use any. It wasn't discipline or strict schedules. It wasn't boarding school, church classes, or educational rigor. It was much more scandalous than that.

In a word, it was love.

She wrote, "People asked me what our secrets were for influencing our children. This is the secret: loving them well, generously, all the time, in every situation."[4]

When I'm not worrying about my eleven-year-old not tying his shoes or my seventeen-year-old not thinking about college, when I'm not worrying about my son's progress in math or my

daughter's advancement in reading, I am left with infinite time to love them. To cherish them. To revel in all the beautiful ways that they are growing and becoming.

When we focus on worry, our days are filled with darkness. When we focus on love, we turn on the light. With the light of love, all the worries and concerns that drag us down are gone.

As filmmaker David Lynch said, we just need to "turn on the light and the darkness goes."[5]

Putting Away Perfection

We stress too much over all the ways we think we're failing our children. As Cindy Rollins, the author of *Mere Motherhood*, said, "Everything we *didn't do* is on a loop before we go to bed."[6]

No, you aren't perfect. You're not going to get it right every week, or even every day for that matter. But you are brave. You are taking on this all-important task of educating your children at home, and there isn't anyone better suited for the task than you.

The real role of parenthood isn't one of manager but moment maker.

It's not being perfect but present.

Not checking all the boxes but embracing the freedom to be real.

It's being aware of our faults but not allowing them to define us.

It's holding space for our kids to be human, stretching ourselves to help them grow.

It's taking the doldrums of every day and working wonders with a little love and creativity.

It's pointing our kids to the light in the midst of darkness and finding beauty in the chaos.

She Is a Gardener

She is a gardener.

She plants and waters, feeds and weeds.

She is curious. She reads and learns and studies the science of growing things. She observes, explores, and experiments like a botanist, playing in her laboratory of living things.

She notices the slightest change in color and condition of the soil. She loves the process, not just the result, and it's made her an explorer of the world.

She smiles as she glances out the window at her garden while she washes dishes. She checks on her little shoots, even when they don't necessarily need anything. She shows up when she's tired or cranky or sick. She's there after a storm or when she returns from a trip. She is nurturing and resilient.

She speaks to her plants, gently of course. One would never shout at a plant. What good would that do? They turn their faces toward the sun and dance in the breeze.

The gardener has learned patience with time, her gentle teacher. Gardening, you see, is a practice in waiting. For nightfall, for the sunrise, for the harvest to come. Through long winters and dry summers and fruitless seasons. The rains fall, the hail destroys, and the sun restores.

There is no one who loves her garden as much as she does, for they did not plant it and they do not tend to it. They might enjoy it, admire it, or even marvel at it. They might ignore it. Some don't really care about growing things, she muses, and that's okay.

Only the hands that have touched a leaf unfurling like a hand slowly opening to praise the sky can love it like she does. Only the brow that has been beaten by the sun while pulling weeds to protect her burgeoning blossoms can really marvel at their becoming. Only the heart that has leapt at the first sprouted seed or the thrill of a second bloom can truly know the wonder of her garden.

Friend, we are more than the ones who gave birth to our babies. We are the gardeners of souls and the sowers of morrows. We are the holders of tears and the keepers of dreams. We are the whisperers of moon-dipped prayers and the protectors of ripening hearts. We are the gardeners, planting seeds of intention and watering them with small acts of love and attention every single day.

I see you, mama.

I see your calloused hands from long days of invisible work. I see your creased eyes from living and loving under a thousand suns. And I see your unspoken hopes like only another mama can.

The gardener is you.

My friend Julie Bogart said that happiness at home is the experience of being okay with our homes the way they are today—unfinished, messy, incomplete—spilling out the sides, running down the legs of the table, and busting through the neatly graphed lines of our schedules.[7]

Whatever you do today, however you feel you're doing in terms of managing your home, taking care of responsibilities, or educating your kids, take time to remember your role.

You can't get it all done, but you can work wonders all the same.

Think about all the hours we waste trying to be the best mother, father, homeschooler, Instagrammer, or fill-in-the blank-er. If we stopped trying to be the best at everything, just imagine how much space we'd have to simply be present. To be perfectly imperfect. To be who we were made to be.

If we focused less on perfection and more on progress, we could stop worrying about how to get it right and just get to it. Get to living. Get to learning. Get to loving.

In the words of Voltaire, "Le mieux est l'ennemi du bien" (The best is the enemy of the good).

So here's to the good life. May your day be filled with hopelessly imperfect, beautifully happy moments. And may you not waste a minute wondering if you got it all right. Because you probably didn't. None of us do, but we go on living and loving anyway.

This holy work of parenthood is never finished.

You Were Made for This

This morning, I awake to the sound of tiny feet pattering down the hallway toward my room and the whispers of dream-drenched children outside my bedroom door. They wait to see if I'm awake, carefully trying to get a peek at my eyes. I don't have to open them to know how close they are.

"She's still asleep," one whispers.

They carefully begin tiptoeing backward toward the door again.

I smile.

They catch it and are in my bed in a flash.

"She's awake!"

"Morning, Mama!"

Laughter and cuddles and morning-breath kisses.

Eventually I climb out from under the covers, a few sets of arms and legs, and a dog who acts offended when I roll her off my chest. I make my way to the kitchen, grind the coffee beans, let the dog out, and begin fulfilling requests for orange juice, waffles, eggs, bagels, and a game of UNO.

After lighting a candle for the breakfast table, I pour a cup of coffee and walk outside to check the garden. The squirrels have been stealing my strawberries at night and digging up seeds. I sigh. Ah, but new sprouts are growing, the sun is shining, and hope is in the air.

Today is going to be a beautiful day.

I breathe a small prayer for the day ahead. For patience, for peace, for good attitudes.

I walk inside to hear bickering. I hush everyone gently and change the subject. The bickering continues. I hum a song, start to clean up the breakfast pans, and wonder if I should wait or ask them to remember: "Is it true? Is it kind? Is it necessary?"

I wait. Where was that patience I asked for?

The arguing continues. I call an audible. "Privileges are hereby revoked until further notice," I say.

Now they're arguing with me. I try not to engage but they know how to push my buttons. I'm running out of patience.

This morning began like most days. Grace. Gratitude. Grand visions of what the day would hold.

And it ended with the feeling that I will never get it right, that I should probably hang up my hat on this whole thing. The homeschooling. The mothering. Who am I fooling, anyway?

Parenting is the hardest thing most of us will ever do. We're all fighting for something different for our kids. Some of us are fighting for their health. Others are fighting for their safety. Many are fighting for their hearts, their souls, and their minds.

Not only are we in a battle for our kids, but we are also at war with ourselves. Our selfish desires, our fatigue, our lack of insight, our unmet expectations, our feelings of inadequacy, and our own childhood trauma are just a few of the enemies we encounter on any given day.

We are imperfect because we are human. But there is no one better suited, more equipped, or tailor-made to be your child's parent than you. No matter who you are, where you came from, or what you're going through today—you were made for this.

If there's anything that life has taught us, it's that parenting is not for the faint of heart. But that's what we do as homeschool parents. We start out with a plan for what we'll do each day: morning time, math lessons, read-alouds, science. But whether those things actually happen is dictated by a number of factors outside our control: bad moods, inclement weather, sickness, a colicky babe on the hip.

Our great challenge is not what we accomplish each day, but how we respond when our plans go awry. Most often, the first thing that comes to mind is that we're failures. We assume this only happens to us, that other moms are teaching Latin and calculus to eager students while *our* toddler is dancing in his own pee and our fifth grader is boycotting math. We know it's silly, but there we sit, wallowing in our despair, until we're ready to quit.

This self-imposed guilt is often compounded by a simple question that's posed by a well-meaning spouse, a relative, or even a curious clerk at the grocery store: "So, what did you accomplish today?"

Let me be the one to tell you that you are not required to account for every bad day you experience. We don't measure our results by a checklist or a to-do list. We measure our results by the lives we are nurturing.

Author Jess Lair once wrote, "Children are not things to be molded, but people to be unfolded."[8]

You cannot possibly rise each day—love your children, educate them the best you know how, and rise again, only to do the same—and be anything less than a success.

You may not see the fruit one day from now, or even one week from now. Months may go by of pouring into these fertile souls without so much as a daisy springing up. But flowers bloom in their own time, each in their own season, according to their unique design.

You are going to make mistakes. Your kids will disappoint you, and you will disappoint your kids. You are going to have days when you can't see the good, and you'll wonder if you made a mistake.

But don't give up.

Creating a life together is messy but oh so worth it. Whether it's twenty minutes or twenty years, you will never regret the time spent together. My prayer is that we would not allow the brokenness of our past and the memories of our mistakes to keep us from a redeemed tomorrow.

So here's to foiled plans, disrupted dreams, and things we never saw coming. Our history may be filled with failure, missteps, and mistakes, but our heritage can be a legacy of love.

One day, our children will look back and remember that their parents weren't perfect. But they will also remember that we loved them well.

Remember

When the days feel long.

When the mud won't wash off.

When no one is listening.

When the kids are bickering, and you're buried in laundry.

Remember to breathe.

Remember to smile.

Remember the good.

Remember the laughter from a failed science experiment or the magic of a read-aloud.

Remember the abundant kisses of your toddler or the rare hug from your teen.

Remember the way they made lunch together or fed the dog (for once).

Remember the love and passion that birthed this journey and just . . . breathe . . . again.

What a beautiful life you're creating.

14

TO SET
THEM FREE

*All people need a place where their
roots can grow deep, and they always
feel like they belong and have a loving
refuge. And all people need a place
that gives wings to their dreams,
nurturing possibilities of who they
might become.*

—SALLY CLARKSON

The day of our children's departure comes too soon. It looms over our heads like an approaching thunderstorm, the clouds gathering in the distance, appearing to barely move at all, until suddenly the rain begins to fall.

"The days are long, but the years are short," as Gretchen Rubin said.[1] So we stretch those days as far as they'll go, knowing full well that our children are growing older with each passing day.

I glanced at my fourteen-year-old the other day, noticed a young man whose voice is deepening, and remembered how it seemed like just yesterday when he was drinking out of a sippy cup.

As the day of departure grows closer, we put so much pressure on ourselves as parents to be prepared for it. To squeeze in all the lessons, experiences, and knowledge they will ever need to be successful in the world. To right all the wrongs and make up for the mistakes before they leave the house. We count on their resiliency to overcome the moments we failed them, and we hold our breath hoping that everything will turn out all right in spite of the opportunities we missed and the heartbreaks they felt.

There's so much joy and beauty on this journey of parenthood, but also so much heartache and regret. For generations, parents all over the world have had the same concern: Are we enough?

The truth is, we are both enough and not enough all at once. As we are learning and growing as parents, we make mistakes and move mountains with equal zeal. But that duality doesn't diminish how our children can or will thrive. Still, the worries are real and can take a tremendous toll on our souls.

"Once upon a midnight dreary, while I pondered, weak and weary," begins Edgar Allan Poe's poem "The Raven." In this story, the narrator is visited by a talking raven. It symbolizes sadness and suffering, the mournful memory of a lost love. By the end of the poem, the raven no longer represents "mournful remembrance" but instead is the embodiment of evil, whose shadow haunts the narrator.

The poem's message is one of caution, to not allow death to lead us to despair. While we may not equate the failures of parenthood to the death of a loved one, our failures can still feel like the death of a dream.

These midnight remembrances are the ravens that haunt our minds and remind us of our misguided longings. In the dark of night, we allow our thoughts to steal the wonder and beauty of our days. When we worry and count our losses, the life we desire becomes nevermore.

We may not be able to prevent these remembrances from creeping into our heads, but we can create a daily ritual of remembering the good. We can overcome the darkness with light.

Lisa Ross, the coauthor of *Simplicity Parenting*, wrote, "The central struggle of parenthood is to let our hopes for our children outweigh our fears."[2]

I've decided to give up worry. It's a habit I have to break, for sure—the hardest one yet. The mind isn't easily swayed. The well-worn paths have grown deeper with frequent travel. I have worn them in well, so I won't be able to tread lightly. I'll have to find a different route altogether.

If I want to succeed, I'll have to adopt a new practice to replace worry. I've chosen gratitude as that practice. It seems obvious enough, but gratitude always takes me to the light. I feel my face physically turning upward as if to soak in all the warmth I can. Gratitude warms me from the inside out. I smile more. I walk more confidently. I trust more easily.

To me, gratitude is hope. And hope, like that small thing with feathers, perches in my soul and rises up in song. It pulls me to the light, draws me close, without asking a thing in return.

Oh, friend, if you've had more bad days than good, more headaches than heart bursts, if the years are waning, and you've reached the end of your rope, please know this: you are not alone. Feel that heartbreak. Breathe it in and grieve it out. I believe we have to let our ideals be shattered before we can get on with the good life. Grief leads to growth, if we only open ourselves to it.

I believe in second chances. I believe in the power of forgiveness and the freedom of truth. I believe mercies are new every morning. I believe each day offers the chance to start again.

And I believe in you.

Make Parent a Noun Again

Once upon a time, we were born with all the parenting instincts we ever needed. But then we heard from the "experts" and read all the books that say otherwise, and we got lost along the way. The way of parenthood has moved from the instinctual to the intellectual, usurping our natural roles.

I suspect this happened because, over the past hundred years, our society moved away from one of survival. It is no longer about giving our children a safe upbringing but about giving them the best life. Now our kids are overmanaged, and we've turned "parent" into a verb.

We are parents. We have children. But to "parent" our children is to try to conform them into who *we* want them to be, rather than help them become who *they* were meant to be.

The use of "parent" as a verb rose in popularity in the 1950s as a way to describe this manufacturing process of turning out kids who act according to our wills.

But parenting is not something we do *to* our children. It's something we do *for* our children when we provide a safe, consistent, healing home in which they can grow strong and vibrant.

I love what Sarah Boyd, of Resilient Little Hearts, said: "Parenthood is a journey toward emotional maturity. It is learning to respond in love when you are hurt, triggered, and overwhelmed. It is learning to love, even when another's behavior is unlovable."[3]

As parents, we are not in the manufacturing business.

If anything, we are gardeners.

Tend the Soil, Not the Seeds

All seasoned gardeners share a special relationship with the soil. They know it's the soil that yields an abundant crop, not merely the seeds themselves.

In *Organic Gardener's Companion*, Jane Shellenberger wrote, "Our most important job as vegetable gardeners is to feed and sustain soil life, often called the soil food web, beginning with the microbes. If we do this, our plants will thrive, we'll grow nutritious, healthy food, and our soil conditions will get better each year. This is what is meant by the adage: 'Feed the soil not the plants.'"[4]

As parents, we tend to nurture the fruit we see in our children. Their passions rising up. Their accomplishments each day. We see something growing, and we want to help it grow bigger. But the source of that beautiful growth lies in the soil, not the sky. Just as soil requires nutrients, water, and air to produce thriving plants, our children need similar things to help them grow strong, healthy, and happy.

"Sufficient, not excessive" is how one gardener puts it. Nothing good comes from excess. A plant's health lies in simplicity and meeting its needs, but not heaping upon it more than it can handle.

The same is true for our children. Just as soil needs air with gaps and room to breathe, our children also need room to grow and move, meditate and heal. And just as soil needs to lie fallow at times in order to become rich with nutrients again, our children have the best chance of becoming healthy, thriving adults when we give them a childhood.

To reawaken wonder in our homes and subsequently our homeschools, we must bring our soil back to life. New growth doesn't spring up from the leaf. It always has and always will begin underground.

Their Lives Will Always Trace Back to You

When I was little, I used to trace the veins on my mother's hands with my fingers. I remember the way they felt beneath my fingertips and how I would try to follow them, like the branches of a willow tree.

This would inevitably make her self-conscious, and she'd tell me that she didn't like how noticeable her veins were. I would look down at my own hands and wonder if hers were once as smooth as mine.

Over the years, she would often tell me I had beautiful hands and how much she loved them. But as I grew, the veins in my hands did too, becoming noticeable with each passing year.

By the time I was a grown woman, it was not lost on me that I had my mother's hands. She always disliked her hands because of the veins that defined them, and for a while, I admit, I felt similarly about mine.

But I remember her hands being so beautiful to me. The way she used them to care for others, visiting dying patients on hospice care or delivering babies in the maternity ward. The way she used them to decorate our home, moving furniture around to create cozy corners, or to make chicken and dumplings from scratch. The way she used them to express herself, pray, or sketch something on paper.

The palms of her hands were smooth and soft, and I remember how soothing they felt when I was sick. How she would hold a cold cloth to my forehead or sit and rub my achy shoulders until I fell asleep. Her hands were strong, graceful, and wise. They were instruments of deep and selfless love.

It was years later that I held her hands in both of mine as a nurse prepared her for brain surgery. She squeezed my hands as hard as she could, although she was incredibly weak. Those beautiful hands, always possessing so much strength, were now frail and thin.

She looked me in the eyes with a wild peace about her: "If it's time to meet my maker," she said with courage, "I want you to know that I am ready."

Her eyes glistened as I shook my head, tears rolling down my cheeks. I couldn't muster the words to speak for fear of becoming completely undone in front of her. But she squeezed my hands again.

"And I need you to let me go, darling."

She smiled and then reached up with her hands to catch my falling tears.

A few short months later, I held her hands again in the back bedroom of our house, only this time she was no longer able to speak or open her eyes. I traced the greenish-blue lines on her hands, those streams of life that would always be a symbol of grace and beauty to me.

This time, it was my turn to speak. I whispered that it was time, that she could let go, but that I would never let her go.

Sometimes I glance down and am surprised to see my mother's hands. I pause as I remember the feel of her smooth touch, her warm, tan skin, and the bold blue veins leading straight to her heart.

I loved my mother's hands, and now my hands. I'm thankful for the prominent veins that define them, like lines on a map leading me back home to the woman I miss so dearly.

Our children will outgrow their childhoods. They'll likely move out of the house, possibly across the country or the world, and have families of their own. They'll build their own lives, and it will feel like they're leaving us behind. But they won't. They can't. Their lives will always trace back to you and me.

 Right now, our calling is to foster those little moments of connection while we have the chance. We often think the magic of childhood is found in the things we give them. The backyard swing sets we build for them. Those unforgettable vacations to theme parks or national parks. And while those are all wonderful things, the magic happens in *you*. And *them*. In the messy mundane of everyday moments.

Make those little investments and just be together. Invest with presence.

If you need peace, create space in your schedule.

If you crave more creativity, carve out time for boredom.

If you long for an adventure, mark it on a calendar and go.

If you desire deeper connection, come together to find common ground.

The profundity of small, simple acts that write a love story is not lost on me. The faithfulness to love our children generously in every situation is not an easy commission. But the reward is great.

Our children grow with our love, not our endless lessons.

They thrive with our trust, not our nagging doubts.

And they become who they were meant to be with our hopes, not our harassment.

Here are two simple questions to guide your days ahead: How are you able to show up in small meaningful ways that will bring a smile to your child's face? And in what ways are you not able to show up? Release the guilt and just be here now.

Rumspringa

My husband grew up in Lancaster County, Pennsylvania, which is known for its Amish population. He used to lie awake at night in his childhood home in the town of Lititz, listening to the sound of horse-drawn buggies clip-clopping down the street. He would wait as the sound of the buggy came closer and closer until he could finally lean over, part the curtain, and watch it go by.

Ben jokes that people ask the Amish the same questions they ask homeschooling families:

"So you teach all your kids in the same room?"

"So you made those clothes yourself?"

"So you named your baby Amos?"

It's easy to poke fun at the Amish way of life, but there are some beautiful parts of their tradition. For example, after a child grows up and leaves the house, a practice called "Rumspringa," the family continues to set a place for him at the table each night, even in his absence. They do this to establish the child's place in the family for all of life.

They say it's why the rate of permanent separation among the Amish is so low. And believe me, separating from a life of no electricity and itchy clothing would be an easy thing to do.

Having such a strong sense of home would have a profound effect on anyone. To go out into the world, sow your wild oats, chase your unrelenting dreams, and act with courage and independence, all the while knowing that your place at the table is still there waiting for you—it would tether your heart to your family and give you something to rely on, no matter what else was going on in the world around you.

The child may leave the family, but the family never leaves the child.

The thought of such a thing nearly takes my breath away.

Isn't that the problem with most families today? Our children grow up together but then go their own way, take separate paths, and sometimes never include each other in the rest of their lives.

We're not Amish. But we've taken a thing or two from them. We will always set a place at the table for our children, even when they are grown and gone. They may leave our home, but home will never leave them.

Set Them Free Even Now

We may have birthed these children, but they do not belong to us. We are merely stewarding them for a season while they're in our care. One day, they'll go out into the world and become who they were meant to be. They'll pursue the dreams that have been germinating in their hearts since birth.

But the act of setting them free begins even now. Not free from our homes or our families, but free to be children in the world.

All of us need a childhood that offers a safe environment, a close connection with our parents or caregivers, plenty of fresh air and physical movement, and the time and space to just be kids.

The renowned educator Maria Montessori composed an anthem for childhood when she declared, "Let the children be free; encourage them, let them run outside when it is raining; let them remove their shoes when they find a puddle of water; and, when the grass of the meadows is damp with dew, let them run on it and trample it with their bare feet, let them rest peacefully when a tree invites them to sleep beneath its shade; let them shout and laugh when the sun wakes them in the morning as it wakes every living creature that divides its day between waking and sleeping."[5]

Whether we experienced such a childhood ourselves says a lot about who we are today. But regardless of our upbringing or how we have raised our children thus far, it is never too late to set our kids free into their own childhoods.

We set them free when we give them time to play and explore. When we give them emotional understanding. When we give them the power of choice. When we give them autonomy over their own bodies. When we give them love and acceptance. And when we let them challenge our authority.

We can set our children free in small but mighty ways

every day, so that by the time they feel ready to leave the nest, it's just one more natural step, not a giant leap of risk and fear.

By contrast, just as we can set our children free, we can strip them of autonomy in small ways, as well. When we dismiss them, rather than validate their feelings. When we think they need discipline when they're merely crying out for attention. When we refuse to move obstacles that would give them a safe place to fall. And when we tell them we love them but fail to show that we really like them.

Setting our children free isn't a final act of farewell. Rather it is a gift we offer them from the moment they are born until our bodies are laid to rest. Freedom is forged from healthy attachment and begins the moment we meet them.

We spend a lifetime setting our children free.

Leave a Legacy of Love

Parents create a legacy through their children. Not through their own success. Not through their accomplishments. Not through their fame or notoriety or standing in the community.

The good news is that you don't need a lot of money to create a rich legacy. All you need is the time, love, and heart for your family.

There is no formula for being wild and free. This is a book of failures and triumphs, of ordinary families daring to break the mold of a cookie-cutter life and create their own adventure.

You have the freedom to carve your own path. If that means using traditional education because that's what your children need, wonderful! If that means working a "regular" job because you really love it and it serves your family's needs, great! If that means your kids participate in team sports because they love it, perfect!

I believe we can leave a great legacy *and* lead an unconventional life.

I believe we can accomplish great things *and* live a great adventure.

I believe we can opt out of conventional systems and still prepare our kids for the real world.

But love is at the heart of everything we do.

Love is the reason we take them outside to explore nature and learn about the world they live in, how to care for it, and all the ways to enjoy it. Love is the reason we read good books to them, sharing the stories of history, classic works of literature, and fantastical worlds to feed their souls, minds, and imaginations.

Love is the reason we let them play, build forts, and create fairy houses. Love is the reason we cultivate curiosity, let them follow their interests, and allow them to become experts in their environments. Love is the reason we seek to keep wonder alive—love for education, but most of all, love for our children.

Love is the reason we believe in childhood.

Love is the reason we are here.

Afterword

t takes courage to live wild and free, to see our children as whole persons, to seek purpose in our learning and living together, to live a life divergent.

Ten years ago, I envisioned a different life for my children. I saw snapshots of family adventures, interest-led learning, and a wild and free childhood. I dreamed of giving them time to grow up and become who they were meant to be.

I've allowed this vision to carry me forth into the unknown. And each year has been an adventure, full of beauty and goodness, missteps and mistakes. But the magic of becoming wild and free is the freedom to try new things, let go of rigid routines, and rediscover our passion for this lifestyle.

Sometimes I think we're crazy for choosing such a different lifestyle from the norm. It would have been so much easier to simply plug into the program and stick with convention. To have regular school hours and designated time together. To have more time for my own interests. To have time to dream and maybe write a novel. To have lunches with friends and adult conversation at the office. To have a clean house and fewer awkward conversations with strangers.

But I could never choose a different path. It might make us a little weird, a little more exhausted, a little different, but it's also what has made our life unforgettable.

Remember that you have a choice in how you spend your one wild and precious life. Society will try to convince you that "experts" have the final say in how your kids will be raised.

But you get to carve your own path for a more meaningful, adventurous life together.

You get to choose how your children grow up: stressed and rushed or slow and peaceful. You get to choose, not to keep them from the world, but to keep out enough of the noise to let them think for themselves.

You get to choose how they learn: at a school or at home, whatever is best for them. You get to travel, take a field trip, or take the day off for rest and restoration.

And you get to choose how you set your children free. You can either weigh them down with the worries of this world or help them see this life as an adventure. You can help them understand that there is no promise of success and that they have permission to make mistakes along the way.

If you're a wild and free family, then you've already made the audacious decision to choose a different path, to live a life divergent. You know that life isn't a pull toward perfection but a pursuit of passion.

Every year of raising our five wild and free children has been an adventure, full of beauty and goodness, but also full of missteps and mistakes.

My prayer is that our incredible out-of-the-box kiddos would always know that successes and failures come hand in hand. That happiness is something we choose, curiosity is something we cultivate, and contentment is a daily commitment as we endeavor to create the life we're dreaming of.

Here's to the ones who are wild and free: the changemakers and homemakers, the fun ones, the crazy ones, the silly and the serious ones. The fearless ones who blaze new trails. The broken ones who keep on going. The old souls and the free spirits. The ones here on Earth and the ones living in our hearts.

When you long to flourish, but it feels like you're floundering . . . when you long for community, but you're drowning in loneliness . . . when you long to see the fruit but all you see is fallow ground—I hope you know that you aren't alone and are so very loved.

Listen for that still, small voice inside you. Remember why you are doing this in the first place: childhood, time, togetherness, and freedom.

May our passion fuel the good fight for our children's futures. May our souls rejoice over every good and beautiful thing about them. May our wholeness hold enough space for the challenges to come.

May goodness and mercy follow them all the days of their lives.

And may they dwell in the refuge of our love now and always.

Acknowledgments

Writing a book about family during a pandemic proved more difficult than I imagined. One would think the world shutting down for a year would be the perfect time to hibernate with a pile of notes and a laptop and blissfully peck out a manuscript.

Only every time I sat down to write about the "wild and free family," I heard a nagging voice say, "Who do you think you are?" or "Look outside your door—there are countless things more important than your little book."

I wanted to give up more than once. The truth is, I threw in the towel multiple times. I just didn't tell my editor. But for better or worse, I always came back again.

Because God, without question.

And because family will always be the answer to a wounded world's cries for healing.

When Mother Teresa was asked what could be done to promote world peace, she answered, "Go home and love your family."

God knows that isn't the easiest answer. But perhaps that is why it is the highest calling.

Family shapes who we are, who we become, and how we live. How we change the world.

I never could have written this without the love, courage, support, and faith of countless others.

First and foremost, my amazing, talented, dream of a husband, Ben. Remember when we had been dating only five months and you sang to me in the middle of a restaurant and then asked me to marry you in front of everyone and I never said yes (because, hello, stunned and speechless introvert here)? Thank you for knowing my answer and taking my hand anyway. For sweeping me off my feet and chasing after dreams with me. For living the impossible and loving the impractical. For offering me the firsts and the lasts and everything in between, always selfless. For giving me the most beautiful, incredible, wonderful children on the planet and honoring the sacred role of motherhood. For being a father who leads by example, always growing, overcoming, and seeking ways to live more vulnerably and authentically for the sake of your family and future generations. For speaking life into my writing. For believing in me, encouraging me, challenging me, and always cheering me on. My cup overflows.

First and secondly (because we're basically hobbits), my awe-inspiring children: Millie, Annie, Cody, Dylan, and Wyatt (in reverse order, just for fun). Your light and love are written into every page. From the moment each of you were born, you have been my teachers. My favorite muses. Each and every day, I am inspired to live braver and love stronger because of you— *for you.* Your ideas, questions, music, stories, laughter, and wisdom are the stuff of life. The joy of my days is living and learning with you. The adventure of your childhoods is only the first chapter of the Great Story of your lives. And each chapter to come is better than the one before, because you belong to the

One who set the moon and the stars in place. Never stop dreaming, believing in magic, or standing up for truth. You are the real wonders of the world. It is my life's greatest honor to be a part of your beautiful becoming. And wherever you go, my heart will always be your home.

To my agent, Alex Field, thank you for taking me under your wing and continuing to champion my passions, ideas, and projects. Your wisdom, warmth, and steady guidance is a gift.

So much gratitude to Katy Hamilton and Chantal Tom for your thoughtfulness, patience, and skill in shaping this book. Your vision, organization, and intentional feedback made a world of difference.

And endless thanks to Judith Curr, Laina Adler, Melinda Mullin, Aly Mostel, Judith Riotto, Julia Kent, and the entire Harper team for taking on this project. You are an absolute dream and it's an honor to be a part of the Harper family.

My heart is full of gratitude for Sally Clarkson, Pam Leo, Julie Bogart, Carla Hannaford, Susan Schaeffer Macaulay, among others whose creative thinking, seasoned wisdom, professional research, and heart work have helped shape many of the beliefs and opinions in this book. Thank you for the incredible gift of your passion and life's work.

To my parents, for shaping so much of who I am today. For giving me my first experience in family. For raising me to believe anything is possible. For giving me a childhood—the good and the hard, the happy and the topsy-turvy, the magical and the free. For doing and giving me your best. I'm so grateful for the pieces of each of you that make me the person I am today.

I owe so much to my extended family and dear friends, who have kept me going. Thank you for your warmth and care over these past gazillion-or-so months. It would take a lifetime to give back in the ways of messages, meals, hugs, and thoughtfulness you have bestowed upon me, but I pray with all my heart I will make it so.

Last but not least, my beloved Wild + Free community. Ten years ago, this community didn't exist, and now hundreds of thousands of mothers, fathers, and families around the world are fighting to save childhood, restore wonder, and reclaim the families they desperately desire. That's because of YOU. Thank you for bravely showing up in your families every single day. When you're tired and weary. When you're sad and defeated. When you're overwhelmed and doubting yourself. When you're fighting for joy like your life depends on it. When you're chasing wonder like your children's futures are at stake.

Courage, dear hearts. One diaper, one meal, one tear-stained pillow. One math lesson, one bath time, one hope-they-sleep-tonight. One book, one prayer, one try-again-tomorrow. One moment, one miracle, one day at a time. I believe we can change the world. I believe we already are.

Notes

Introduction: Your Family Was Made for More

1. Cindy Rollins, Wild + Free conference, Franklin, TN, September 18, 2020.
2. Dylan Thomas, "Do Not Go Gentle into That Good Night," *Dylan Thomas Selected Poems, 1934–1952* (New York: New Directions, 2003), 122.

Chapter 2: To Preserve Childhood

1. Charlotte Mason, *The Original Homeschooling Series* (New York: Simon and Schuster, 2013), 42.
2. Joseph Chilton Pearce, *Magical Child* (New York: Penguin Publishing Group, 1992), 14.
3. Peter Gray, "Give Childhood Back to Children," *Independent*, January 12, 2014, https://www.independent.co.uk/voices/comment/give-childhood -back-to-children-if-we-want-our-offspring-to-have-happy-productive -and-moral-lives-we-must-allow-more-time-for-play-not-less-are-you -listening-gove-9054433.html.
4. Marie Winn, "The Loss of Childhood," *New York Times*, May 8, 1983, https://www.nytimes.com/1983/05/08/magazine/the-loss-of-child hood.html.
5. Winn, "The Loss of Childhood."
6. "Internet Statistics," GuardChild, n.d., https://www.guardchild.com /statistics.
7. "Suicide in Children and Teens," American Academy of Child and Adolescent Psychiatry, updated June 2021, https://www.aacap.org/AACAP /Families_and_Youth/Facts_for_Families/FFF-Guide/Teen-Suicide -010.aspx.

8. Winn, "The Loss of Childhood."

9. This has been paraphrased from Mother Teresa, "Nobel Lecture," Nobel Peace Prize acceptance speech, December 11, 1979, https://www.nobel prize.org/prizes/peace/1979/teresa/lecture/.

10. Bruce Perry, *The Body's Most Fascinating Organ: The Brain*, Chicago Ideas, December 10, 2013, Edison Talks video, 17:42, https://www.chicagoideas .com/videos/the-body-s-most-fascinating-organ-the-brain.

Chapter 3: To Connect with Your Kids

1. Tillie Olsen, *Silences* (New York: Feminist Press at CUNY, 2014), https:// www.google.com/books/edition/Silences/ouHSAwAAQBAJ?hl =en&gbpv=1&dq=%E2%80%9Cmotherhood+means+being+instantly +interruptible,+responsive,+responsible,%E2%80%9D&pg=PT67& printsec=frontcover.

2. Pam Leo, *Connection Parenting: Parenting Through Connection Instead of Coercion, Through Love Instead of Fear* (Deadwood, OR: Wyatt-MacKenzie, 2005), 21.

3. Leo, *Connection Parenting*, 20.

4. Jean Piaget, "Adult Constraint and Moral Realism," chap. 2 in *The Moral Judgment of the Child* (London: Routledge, 1932).

5. Sally Clarkson, "Cultivating Friendship with Children and Podcast," *Sally Clarkson* (blog), July 23, 2019, https://sallyclarkson.com/blog/2019/6/23 /restoring-your-life-podcast-friendship-with-children.

6. Leo, *Connection Parenting*, 87.

7. "About Connection Parenting," Connection Parenting, 2020, https:// connectionparenting.com/about.

8. "About Connection Parenting," https://connectionparenting.com/about.

9. Vince Gowmon, "4 Reasons I Take Issue with Teaching Children Medita- tion in School," *Vince Gowmon* (blog), n.d., https://www.vincegowmon .com/4-reasons-i-take-issue-with-teaching-children-meditation-in-school/.

10. Leo, *Connection Parenting*, 38.

11. Alfie Kohn, *Unconditional Parenting: Moving from Rewards and Punishments to Love and Reason* (New York: Atria Books, 2005), 20.

12. Betsy Jenkins's Instagram: https://www.instagram.com/homeschooling _withtheclassics/?hl=en.

13. Isa. 40:31 (NIV).

Chapter 4: To Understand Your Children

1. Harry S. Truman, Forbes Quotes, n.d., https://www.forbes.com/quotes /3860/.

2. Po Bronson and Ashley Merryman, *NurtureShock: New Thinking About Children* (New York: Twelve, 2009), 6.

3. "9 Words for Types of Parenting," Merriam-Webster, updated March 25, 2022, https://www.merriam-webster.com/words-at-play/types-of-parents-meanings.

4. "Laurie Buchanan Quotes," Goodreads, n.d., https://www.goodreads.com/author/quotes/1338073.Laurie_Buchanan.

5. Thomas Armstrong, *Awakening Genius in the Classroom* (Alexandria, VA: Association for Supervision and Curriculum Development, 1998), 67.

6. Armstrong, *Awakening Genius in the Classroom*, 2.

7. Courtney Campbell, "Alumna Performs Dream Role in 'Wicked,'" Elon News Network, January 12, 2016, https://www.elonnewsnetwork.com/article/2016/01/alumna-performs-dream-role-on-wicked.

8. "Benjamin West," Wikipedia, last modified February 12, 2022, https://en.wikipedia.org/wiki/Benjamin_West.

9. Armstrong, *Awakening Genius in the Classroom*.

10. Florence Littauer, AZQuotes.com, Wind and Fly LTD, 2022, https://www.azquotes.com/quote/1416968.

11. Leon F. Seltzer, "Feeling Understood—Even More Important Than Feeling Loved?," *Psychology Today*, June 28, 2017, https://www.psychologytoday.com/us/blog/evolution-the-self/201706/feeling-understood-even-more-important-feeling-loved.

12. George Orwell, *1984* (London: Secker & Warburg, 1949), 318.

13. Brené Brown, *Daring Greatly: How the Courage to Be Vulnerable Transforms the Way We Live, Love, Parent, and Lead* (New York: Penguin Books, 2013).

Chapter 5: To Create a Safe Haven

1. Bruce Perry, *The Body's Most Fascinating Organ: The Brain*, Chicago Ideas, December 10, 2013, Edison Talks video, 17:42, https://www.chicagoideas.com/videos/the-body-s-most-fascinating-organ-the-brain.

2. Susan Schaeffer Macaulay, *For the Family's Sake: The Value of Home in Everyone's Life* (Wheaton, IL: Crossway, 1999).

3. T. S. Eliot, "East Coker," *Four Quartets*, part 5, line 19.

4. 1 Cor. 13:4–5 (NIV).

Chapter 6: To Redeem What's Been Broken

1. Pam Leo, *Connection Parenting: Parenting Through Connection Instead of Coercion, Through Love Instead of Fear* (Deadwood, OR: Wyatt-MacKenzie, 2005), 33.

2. Laura Markham, "How to Handle Your Anger at Your Child," *Psychology Today*, May 11, 2016, https://www.psychologytoday.com/us/blog/peaceful-parents-happy-kids/201605/how-handle-your-anger-your-child.

3. Andrew Curry, "Parents' Emotional Trauma May Change Their Children's Biology. Studies in Mice Show How," *Science*, July 18, 2019, https://www .science.org/content/article/parents-emotional-trauma-may-change -their-children-s-biology-studies-mice-show-how.
4. Karina Margit Erdelyi, "Can Trauma Be Passed Down from One Generation to the Next?," Psycom, March 31, 2020, https://www.psycom.net /epigenetics-trauma.
5. Dr. Gabor Maté, "Dr. Gabor Maté on the Connection Between Stress and Disease," YouTube, August 15, 2019, YouTube video, 1:16:45, https://www .youtube.com/watch?v=ajo3xkhTbfo.
6. Will Cole (@drwillcole), "What would have seemed science fiction not too long ago . . . ," Instagram photo, November 13, 2021, https://www .instagram.com/p/CWO7O6xv9ro.
7. Leo, *Connection Parenting*, 33.
8. Nikol Chen, "The Present You Are Constructing Should Look Like the Future You Are Dreaming," Laidlaw Scholars, February 8, 2021, https:// laidlawscholars.network/posts/the-present-you-are-constructing- should-look-like-the-future-you-are-dreaming?room_id=1283- leadership-quote-of-the-week.
9. L. R. Knost—Little Hearts/Gentle Parenting Resources, Facebook, November 6, 2019, https://www.facebook.com/littleheartsbooks/photos /we-have-to-break-the-cycle-of-hurting-children-to-raise-children-hurting -childre/2722210974476156/.

Chapter 7: To Chase Wonder

1. Jane Goodall and Douglas Abrams, *The Book of Hope: A Survival Guide for an Endangered Planet* (New York: Viking, 2021).
2. Goodall and Abrams, *The Book of Hope*.
3. "About Jane," Jane Goodall Institute, n.d., https://janegoodall.org/our -story/about-jane/.
4. Katrien Van Deuren, Wild + Free content bundles, October 2019.
5. Victoria L. Dunckley, "Nature's Rx: Green-Time's Effects on ADHD," *Psychology Today*, June 20, 2013, https://www.psychologytoday.com/us /blog/mental-wealth/201306/natures-rx-green-times-effects-adhd.
6. Pasi Sahlberg and William Doyle, *Let the Children Play: For the Learning, Well-Being, and Life Success of Every Child* (Oxford: Oxford University Press, 2020), 344.
7. Katrina Schwartz, "Why Kids Need to Move, Touch, and Experience to Learn," KQED, March 26, 2015, https://www.kqed.org/mindshift/39684 /why-kids-need-to-move-touch-and-experience-to-learn.
8. Laura DePriest, "How Multisensory Activities Enhance Reading Skills,"

Edutopia, June 18, 2021, https://www.edutopia.org/article/how-multi
sensory-activities-enhance-reading-skills.

9. Jean Piaget, "Some Aspects of Operations," in *Play and Development: A
Symposium with Contributions by Jean Piaget, Peter H. Wolff, Rene A. Spitz,
Konrad Lorenz, Lois Barclay Murphy, Erik H. Erikson*, ed. Maria W. Piers
(New York: W. W. Norton, 1972), 27.

10. Kendra Cherry, "Jean Piaget Quotes," Verywell Mind, updated June 10,
2021, https://www.verywellmind.com/jean-piaget-quotes-2795116.

11. "Robert Frost Quotable Quote," Goodreads, n.d., https://www.goodreads
.com/quotes/50818-i-am-not-a-teacher-but-an-awakener.

12. "Albert Einstein Quotable Quote," Goodreads, n.d., https://www.good
reads.com/quotes/1038525-be-a-loner-that-gives-you-time-to-wonder-to.

13. E. Merrill Root, "Quote of the Day," School of Practical Philosophy, n.d.,
https://practicalphilosophy.org.au/we-need-a-renaissance-of-wonder
-we-need-to-renew-in-our-hearts-and-in-our-souls-the-deathless-dream
-the-eternal-poetry-the-perennial-sense-that-life-is-miracle-and-magic
-e-merrill-root/.

14. Sally Clarkson, *Awaking Wonder: Opening Your Child's Heart to the Beauty
of Learning* (Bloomington, MN: Bethany House Publishers, 2020), 117.

15. Christine Cooper, "Nature Study," *Parents' Review* 20 (1909): 337–48.

16. James Joyce, *Ulysses* (Paris: Shakespeare and Company, 1922).

17. Brian Greene, "Put a Little Science in Your Life," *New York Times*, June 1,
2008, https://www.nytimes.com/2008/06/01/opinion/01greene.html.

18. Bertrand Russell, "In Praise of Idleness," *Harper's Magazine*, October
1932, https://harpers.org/archive/1932/10/in-praise-of-idleness.

19. Clarkson, *Awaking Wonder*, 154.

Chapter 8: To Adventure Together

1. The Bigfoot Field Researchers Organization website: https://www. bfro.net.

2. Matt Blitz, "I Found Bigfoot . . . Maybe," *Popular Mechanics*, July 17, 2019,
https://www.popularmechanics.com/adventure/outdoors/a28401253
/is-bigfoot-real.

3. Greta Eskridge, *Adventuring Together: How to Create Connections and Make
Lasting Memories with Your Kids* (Nashville, TN: Nelson Books, 2020), 118.

4. "Helen Keller 1180–1968," Oxford Reference, n.d., https://www.oxford
reference.com/view/10.1093/acref/9780191826719.001.0001/q-oro
ed4-00006224.

5. Fell & Fair Instagram account: https://www. instagram.com/fellandfair.

6. Roald Dahl, *My Year* (New York: Viking Juvenile, 1994), 56.

Chapter 9: To Unleash Their Gifts

1. Jia Tolentino, "The Repressive, Authoritarian Soul of 'Thomas the Tank Engine & Friends,'" *The New Yorker*, September 28, 2017, https://www .newyorker.com/culture/rabbit-holes/the-repressive-authoritarian-soul -of-thomas-the-tank-engine-and-friends.
2. Kim John Payne and Lisa M. Ross, *Simplicity Parenting: Using the Extraordinary Power of Less to Raise Calmer, Happier, and More Secure Kids* (New York: Ballantine Books, 2010), 180.
3. Marc Brackett, *Permission to Feel: Unlocking the Power of Emotions to Help Our Kids, Ourselves, and Our Society Thrive* (New York: Celadon, 2019), 126.
4. Brackett, *Permission to Feel*, 127.
5. Brackett, *Permission to Feel*, 143.
6. Ben Cichy (@bencichy), Twitter, November 22, 2019, 12:44 a.m., https:// www.twitter.com/bencichy/status/1197752802929364992?lang=en.
7. Celeste Headlee, *Do Nothing: How to Break Away from Overworking, Overdoing, and Underliving* (New York: Harmony, 2020), xvii.
8. Blaise Pascal, *Pensées* (France, 1669), https://www.google.com/books /edition/Pens%C3%A9es_by_Blaise_Pascal/ZpyczgEACAAJ?hl=en.
9. Nicholas Carr, *The Shallows: What the Internet Is Doing to Our Brains* (New York: W. W. Norton, 2020).
10. Paige Leskin, "American Kids Want to Be Famous on YouTube, and Kids in China Want to Go to Space: Survey," *Business Insider*, July 17, 2019, https://www.businessinsider.com/american-kids-youtube-star-astronauts -survey-2019-7.
11. "Margaret Wise Brown Quotes," Goodreads, n.d., https://www.goodreads .com/author/quotes/18479.Margaret_Wise_Brown.
12. Charlotte Mason, *Home Education* (n.p.: Living Book Press, 2017), 44.
13. Payne and Ross, *Simplicity Parenting*, 143.
14. Tim Kreider quoted in Ferris Jabr, "Why Your Brain Needs More Downtime," *Scientific American*, October 15, 2013, https://www.scientific american.com/article/mental-downtime.
15. Aja Lake, "The Less-Is-More Rules of 'Simplicity Parenting,'" *Mother*, February 10, 2016, https://www.mothermag.com/simplicity-parenting/.
16. Payne and Ross, *Simplicity Parenting*, 34.
17. Jo Boaler, *Limitless Mind: Learn, Lead, and Live Without Barriers* (New York: HarperOne, 2019), 220.

Chapter 10: To Unlock Their Potential

1. Lindsay Mumma, "On Their Own: How to Stop Interfering with Your Child's Development," *Pathways to Family Wellness*, no. 61, March 1, 2019, https://pathwaystofamilywellness.org/Children-s-Health-Wellness

/on-their-own-how-to-stop-interfering-with-your-childs-development
.html.

2. Robert Melillo, *Reconnected Kids: Help Your Child Achieve Physical, Mental, and Emotional Balance* (New York: Perigee, 2011), 28.
3. Melillo, *Reconnected Kids*, 27.
4. Bette Lamont, "Signs and Symptoms of NeuroDevelopmental Gaps," Neuro-Developmental Movement, https://www.neurodevelopmentalmovement.org/articles/signs-and-symptoms-of-neurodevelopmental-gaps/.
5. Daniel J. Siegel and Tina Payne Bryson, *The Whole-Brain Child: 12 Revolutionary Strategies to Nurture Your Child's Developing Mind* (New York: Bantam Books, 2012), 7.

Chapter 11: To Pursue a Vision

1. Suzanne Raga, "25 of History's Greatest Moms," Mental Floss, May 8, 2016, https://www.mentalfloss.com/article/79143/25-historys-greatest-moms.
2. Raga, "25 of History's Greatest Moms."
3. "Mothers of Famous People," *Deseret News*, May 12, 2006, https://www.deseret.com/2006/5/12/19952872/mothers-of-famous-people.

Chapter 12: To Become Together

1. Flora Merrill, "A Short Story Course Can Only Delay, It Cannot Kill an Artist, Says Willa Cather," in *Willa Cather in Person: Interviews, Speeches, and Letters*, ed. L. Brent Bohlke (Lincoln, NE: University of Nebraska Press, 1986), https://cather.unl.edu/writings/bohlke/interviews/bohlke.i.21.
2. Pam Leo, *Connection Parenting: Parenting Through Connection Instead of Coercion, Through Love Instead of Fear* (Deadwood, OR: Wyatt-MacKenzie, 2005), 71.

Chapter 13: To Not Grow Weary

1. Atticus, "The doubters are just dreamers with broken hearts," Twitter, November 12, 2021, https://twitter.com/atticuspoetry/status/1459251654067429376?lang=en.
2. Renee Huston, Wild + Free content bundles, September 2020.
3. Richele Baburina, Wild + Free simulcast conference, Franklin, TN, September 19, 2020.
4. Sally Clarkson, *Awaking Wonder: Opening Your Child's Heart to the Beauty of Learning* (Bloomington, MN: Bethany House Publishers, 2020).
5. David Lynch, *Catching the Big Fish: Meditation, Consciousness, and Creativity* (New York: Penguin, 2007), 98.

6. Cindy Rollins, Wild + Free conference, Franklin, TN, September 28, 2019.
7. Julie Bogart, *The Brave Learner: Finding Everyday Magic in Homeschool, Learning, and Life* (New York: Penguin Publishing Group, 2019), 10.
8. Jess Lair, AZQuotes.com, Wind and Fly LTD, 2022, https://www .azquotes.com/quote/1016012.

Chapter 14: To Set Them Free

1. Gretchen Rubin, "Secret of Adulthood: The Days Are Long, but the Years Are Short," *Gretchen Rubin* (blog), May 27, 2014, https:// gretchenrubin.com/2014/05/secret-of-adulthood-the-days-are-long -but-the-years-are-short/.
2. Kim John Payne and Lisa M. Ross, *Simplicity Parenting: Using the Extraordinary Power of Less to Raise Calmer, Happier, and More Secure Kids* (New York: Ballantine Books, 2010), 27.
3. Sarah Boyd (@resilientlittlehearts), "Parenthood is a journey . . . ," Instagram photo, February 18, 2021, https://www.instagram.com/p/CLcp7xU BAZa.
4. Jane Shellenberger, *Organic Gardener's Companion: Growing Vegetables in the West* (Golden, Colorado: Fulcrum Publishing, 2012).
5. Simone Davies, *The Montessori Toddler: A Parent's Guide to Raising a Curious and Responsible Human Being* (New York: Workman Publishing Group, 2019), 60.

About Wild + Free

Henry David Thoreau wrote, "All good things are wild and free." This quote is the inspiration for the Wild + Free community because it represents a growing movement of parents, educators, and caregivers who want their children not only to receive a quality education, but also to experience the adventure, freedom, and wonder of childhood.

LEARN MORE ABOUT WILD + FREE

Website: bewildandfree.org
Instagram: @wildandfree.co
Facebook: facebook.com/bewildandfree
Conferences: members.bewildandfree.org/conferences
The Wild + Free Farm Village: bewildandfree.org/farmvillage
Wild + Free Podcast: soundcloud.com/bewildandfree
Wild + Free Content Bundles: bewildandfree.org/bundles
Wild + Free Groups: bewildandfree.org/about-groups

Find more ideas, activities, and ways to become a
Wild + Free family here:

Available wherever books, e-books, and audiobooks are sold
DISCOVER GREAT AUTHORS, EXCLUSIVE OFFERS, AND MORE AT HC.COM.